Learning Centre

City and Islington College
Marlborough Building
383 Holloway Road N7 0RN
tel. 020 7700 9283

CITY AND ISLINGTON
COLLEGE

For a catalogue of related titles
in our Sexual Politics/Global Issues list
please write to us at the address below.

Cassell
Wellington House
125 Strand
London WC2R 0BB

127 West 24th Street
New York, NY 10011

© Turan Ali

First published 1996

British Library Cataloguing-in-Publication Data
A catalogue record for this book is available from the British Library.

ISBN 0-304-33148-1 (hardback)
       0-304-33150-3 (paperback)

Typeset by Ben Cracknell Studios
Printed and bound in Great Britain by Biddles Ltd,
Guildford and King's Lynn

Contents

Author's note

All the names of parents and children mentioned in this book have been changed to protect their identities. The towns have also been changed. Although not all the people interviewed asked for anonymity, the majority did, so it seemed sensible to use pseudonyms throughout. When partners are introduced, e.g. as 'Mark, 40, and Hassan, 31,' it is the first-mentioned whose words follow, unless otherwise indicated.

Lesbian mothers are the most-often-talked-about section of the 'lesbian and gay parent' community. Although there has been no significant research on the numbers of lesbian and gay parents, the many hundreds of people contacted in the research for this book have left me in no doubt that there are hundreds of thousands of lesbian and gay people in the UK who have parented children.

It has also become clear that perhaps the majority of lesbian and gay parents still achieve parenthood through a former or still current (apparently) heterosexual relationship or marriage, and that there are massive numbers of both lesbian women and gay men who are parents through these routes to parenthood. Consequently, this book focuses on as wide a range as possible of lesbian and gay people who are parents.

Foreword

When I first told my father I was queer he asked if anyone had 'interfered' with me as a choirboy in the local parish church. To this day the corruption theory of homosexuality remains surprisingly pervasive. Gay sex, according to the logic of this view, is sensational: try it once and you're hooked for life. Actually I can recall sexual fantasies about other boys – and older men – from the age of four or five, while at eleven I'd have liked nothing better than a little 'interference' from fellow members of the all-male church choir. They were, alas, mostly straight – and those who weren't never gave me a second glance. So much for corruption.

Mention lesbian or gay parents to the average het Brit, however, and the C-word will hover, spoken or unspoken, over the remainder of your conversation. With homosexual role models, what chance will the poor tykes have of growing up 'normal'? The answer of course is exactly the same chance as anyone else.

Years of pressure from parents, siblings, schoolfriends, soaps, comics, magazines, movies, advertising and pop lyrics consistently fail to make gay teenagers grow up straight. Experience suggests that hets will be het, queers will be queer and there's not a damn thing parents – or anyone else – can do about it.

Actually lesbians and gays often make rather good mothers and fathers – not to mention teachers, youth leaders and counsellors – because we know at first hand how far the needs of a child may differ from the expectations of its parents. 'Be yourself' should be the first tenet not only of gay liberation, but of growing up itself.

There are already too many disturbed and wretched children in schools across our country. Making babies is the work of moments, undertaken all too lightly by the reckless, the immature and the downright irresponsible. Lesbians and gays who become parents don't – on the whole – do so by accident; every mother is willing, every child is wanted.

My own son is just five, which makes me no kind of expert on parenthood. For years I always found other people's babies and children rather daunting, and 'breeder' was a favourite term of abuse used to make fun of heterosexuals behind their backs. Naturally enough, having a kid of my own changed all that – I now find myself flirting with babies in prams and stopping their parents in the street to coo and flatter. It's nauseating.

Parenthood is certainly stressful and maybe worse is still to come, yet when a small person spontaneously flings his arms around your neck and calls you 'darling daddy' the feeling is incomparable. Most of us are replaceable at work or at play, but no one will ever replace you as that child's parent. This relationship is for life.

Forget sexuality. Happy, secure kids need happy, secure parents willing to embrace the decades of commitment, love and support that are every infant's birthright. The traditional nuclear family has no monopoly on these qualities. Everyone who can bring them to bear in raising the next generation will deserve its undying thanks.

Tom Robinson

Preface

Many lesbians, gay men and bisexuals are parents. Many have created healthy, stable and nurturing family units involving either or both of the natural parents with their same-sex partners as co-parents. Most of them hide the full facts to some extent. This is not surprising given the myths and prejudices in modern society, which are many and virulent, about any homosexual adult being involved in child-rearing. Lesbian, gay and bisexual parents are, according to these myths, unsuitable as parents because they are likely to sexually abuse their children; they will ensure their children grow up to be homosexual; and their children will lead miserable lives riddled with persecution, emotional turmoil and deep confusion over their gender roles and identities and their sexuality: such is the folklore.

This book, largely through the personal testimonies of lesbian, gay and bisexual parents, shows that these myths are false. In fact, the opposite of these prejudices is usually true. The latest research shows that children brought up by same-sex couples or non-heterosexual extended families develop well-balanced and emotionally stable personalities, are confident and clear about their gender roles and identities, exhibit a diverse range of sexualities (no different from the range exhibited by children of heterosexual families) and have a more positive attitude towards their parents and their parents' partners. And as for child abuse, it is very largely the domain of the more traditional, heterosexual upbringing so applauded by critics of lesbian, gay and bisexual parents.

As the testimonies show, *because* of the prejudice lesbian, gay and bisexual parents know they will face to some degree, they have thought through and catered for a much wider range of practical, emotional and educational issues than the average heterosexual couple. Whatever one's prejudices or preconceptions about lesbian, gay or bisexual parents, this book will hopefully show that children born to homosexual parents (or non-heterosexual extended families) are likely to have a pretty good start in life.

This book does not claim to reflect statistically the numbers of lesbian, gay and bisexual parenting arrangements that exist in Britain. However, it does reflect the most common ways in which non-heterosexuals form family units and conceive and rear children in the UK. It should also be noted that perhaps the largest numbers of lesbian and gay parents are still in apparently heterosexual marriages or relationships, or at least conceived their children while in such a situation, although no extensive research has been done to estimate the numbers involved. The graphic, sometimes violent and shocking experiences of some of the families interviewed are the extreme products of a much more common phenomenon; namely, the problems caused by heterosexuals, be they relatives, neighbours or bureaucrats, who cannot accept or tolerate homosexual adults being parents. One wonders how they would react if they discovered that lesbian, gay and bisexual parents often do a better job. Please lend them your copy of this book.

All the parents whose stories are included in this book and the countless other lesbian, gay and bisexual parents in the UK have every right to be proud of their achievements and to have their experiences documented in this book.

'Queers make fab parents.'
(Lisa, 19, heterosexual daughter of two lesbian mothers)

Acknowledgements

My thanks go to the many lesbian, gay and bisexual parents, grandparents and their children who so generously and honestly allowed me to poke around in their family histories. I hope the book does justice to the courage, integrity and love that I have witnessed time and again in the many healthy and happy lesbian and gay families who are a part of this book. I am also indebted to the hundreds of people whom I chased, persuaded and tracked down, who I had been told knew a gay, lesbian or bisexual person who was a parent. I know there were delicate negotiations to get agreement for some of those interviews and I am very grateful.

Special thanks go to Catherine Hopper, who conducted a significant number of the interviews, with tact, precision and warmth. Thanks also to that wonderful resource of lesbian and gay studies, which has a global archive of our lives and experiences, Homodok (Amsterdam University); and warmest thanks to André Ancion for research, love and support, Michael Raymond for the interview transcriptions, and to my wonderful partner, Iain Hay, who really understands the meaning of commitment.

For my mother (even though she isn't a lesbian)

ONE

Come out, Come out, Wherever You Are

Lesbian, gay and bisexual parents have been around forever. In the past they were virtually all cloaked in heterosexual marriages, but in recent decades they have progressively been living the lives that legislation and social attitudes did not allow before. This first chapter introduces a wide range of routes to lesbian, gay and bisexual parenthood, representing both the well-known and the less-expected ways that non-heterosexual family units are created. Inevitably, many of these family units are created in the aftermath of coming out within an apparently heterosexual marriage. However, there are so many ingenious, planned and accidental arrivals at parenthood that the whole book could have been filled with the surprising, shocking and touching stories of 'how we came to be parents'.

Sally, 26, with her lover Jan, 28, are mothers to Lucy, 2. *Manchester.*

We'd been going to our local lesbian and gay social group for months and had met a lot of really nice people. But it wasn't until we started talking about having a child ourselves that we found out a lot of the lesbians and gay men there were parents, either from a previous marriage or a teenage experiment, from artificial insemination or by being a donor, or as a co-parent, and in one case, through fostering. What amazed us was how many different types were parents, the trendies as well as the cardigans, and that so many of them hadn't mentioned it until we brought up the subject.

Maggie, 36, and Shelley, 40, mothers to twins, 4. *London.*

We met just after the children were born. My previous relationship was breaking up at the time. I was having to juggle two babies and try to forget that my partner was out with another woman. When I met Shelley we fell in love very quickly; I can't imagine why. I looked completely washed out after weeks of coping on my own with twin babies. Shelley finally moved in when the kids were about six months old. The twins are four now and as we both work long hours we have a full-time nanny, living at home during the week with us, and it's fab! Not the set-up you expect for lesbian parents, eh?

Samantha, 39, mother to two adult daughters, 19 and 23, and co-parent, with her lover Stella, 28, to Holly, 2. *Kent.*

I was in a straight marriage for eighteen years. It was horrendous. My husband locked me out of the house, beat me, trashed my possessions and much, much more. He even convinced my doctor that I needed help and got me put in a psychiatric hospital. When we got there, they decided *he* needed help not me, and he ran off. It didn't help when he found out about my sexuality. I told him. I also said I couldn't handle being with him any more and I was going to leave him. A couple weeks later he decided I'd be better off dead. He'd taken me out for the evening, I was driving my car, and on the way home he asked if I'd enjoyed myself. I said, 'Yes.' He said that meant I wouldn't leave him. When I told him it didn't make any difference, he grabbed the wheel and steered us into the oncoming traffic while kicking and punching me. I managed to stop the car and, as I took my foot off the brake, he pushed me out of the driver's door, punching me in the face and knocking out my front teeth. He got in the driver's seat and started reversing over me. He didn't get me. I got up and ran. I put my teeth in my pocket, I don't know why. I wandered around for a few hours before I went home to find he'd ripped up my coursework and destroyed all my tapes (I was doing a Women's Studies course at the time). I moved out the next day. He's never ever mentioned the beating he gave me. I left the marriage, and the youngest of my two daughters came to live with me. My older daughter decided to stay with him. A few weeks later he followed me to Stella's place and he was incredibly reasonable and said he hoped she would make me happy and that he'd sorted out a house for us. We didn't believe it, but we had to move out of Stella's flat, so we had no choice but to move into the house he'd got for us. The house turned out to be a squat and there was no electricity. It was up for sale and he'd copied the keys from the estate agent and had broken in that way. Thankfully, after three weeks he finally agreed to move out of the family house. What I didn't know was the house was about to be re-possessed because he'd got a second mortgage on it by forging my signature. Stella and I'll be paying off the debts for years to come; the house'll probably never be ours. He's been back since we've been divorced and smacked me in the face, threatened our younger daughter and dragged her off screaming, thrown furniture around like paper. Stella called the police. They said they couldn't do anything because it was a 'domestic'. What upsets me is that my eldest daughter doesn't regard me as mum, and she sees her father as perfect. She believes his side of the story and doesn't speak to Stella at all. She blames her for breaking up the marriage, which isn't true. He is convinced that I will wake up one day and go back to him. 'We're nearly back together,' he said to me recently. 'In your wildest dreams!' I told him. Now I'm building a stable, loving family with Stella and our daughter, Holly, who's just turned two. This is how it should be, a caring, peaceful, safe home; not the hell I had with my ex-husband.

Jim, 38, single father to Hayley, 8. *Isle of Wight.*

Jack and I had spent twelve months working together on shifts in the City and became very good friends. I decided our friendship should be based on truth so I told him I was gay. He was then a married man with two kids. When I first met him I didn't like him, he was very 'Eastendish', but as the friendship developed he admitted his marriage was a sham and his mother had pushed him into it. For about a year after I came out to him he was colder towards me and distant, but then one Saturday afternoon he came over to my flat and said, 'Can I move in with you?' We had no sexual relationship at this point and I was hesitant because he'd just left his wife, so I said, 'No.' At six o'clock that evening he turned up with a suitcase having had a row with his mum and he had nowhere else to go. We ended up in bed that evening. Five years into the relationship we decided we wanted kids. Me because I can't accept that being gay means you can't have kids and Jack because he was already a father but didn't have custody of his kids, and there was no way he was going to get custody of them. It was in my heart I wanted to be a father. Jack and I moved into a house in small-town-nowhere because it was all we could afford in the late 1980s property boom. It took two years of advertising for a surrogate mother, just someone who was healthy and sensible; we weren't looking for a perfect mother. I come from a middle-class background, his is macho working-class, we thought it would be very frowned upon to have a surrogate mother. We also never thought we'd achieve it. We never thought the right person would come along but in the end it all worked out. Four days after the baby was born the mother had no more contact with Hayley, although she stayed with us for a year as a lodger before moving on. Of course we 'set her up' with her own place as a way of saying thank you. I don't think she could believe her luck.

Julie, 24, mother to Ben, 4, whom she co-parents with part-time father, Joe. *Blackpool.*

I joined a lesbian social group 'cos I wanted to meet more dykes and find out more about having kids. I wanted to do it safely but I wasn't sure how to go about it all. My lover, Kath, was reluctant at first 'cos she thought they'd all be snobs. And she was right. They were all so middle-class and talked down to us. At least I thought they were. It was funny 'cos Kath started telling me I was over-reacting when it was her that didn't want to go in the first place. Anyway, in the end I became so pissed off with the wanky discussions about childcare and maternity leave that we stopped going. I mean, Kath and I were both unemployed, I've got no qualifications and I've only ever had a few temporary jobs so nannies and 'career breaks' weren't exactly what we needed to talk about. In the end we got so impatient that I asked Joe, a friend of my brother, to be the donor father. No medical tests, no contracts, nothing. Joe didn't want anything to do with bringing up the baby so I didn't ask any questions. When Kath and I split up when I was seven months pregnant, I couldn't believe how brilliant Joe was. He really got into the idea of being a dad. He didn't want the kid himself or anything but he helped out sometimes with cash and baby-sitting. He still does. I haven't told the Child Support Agency who the father is, that was the deal with Joe, but they don't think there's anything strange about someone like me being a single mum 'cos of a one-night stand . . . that's how my mum had me!

Glenda, 31, who co-parents with Sally, 40, their daughter Nerys, 4. *Southampton.*

My parents run a pub and I lived and worked with them until my early twenties. One day mum found my copy of *Spare Rib*[1] with some contact ads ringed. She said, 'If ever you turn out like that, don't worry. You can come and talk to me.' So, five weeks after meeting Sally I moved her into the pub. Mum knew Sally was gay but she didn't seem to understand the full picture. When I decided I would leave the pub 'cos Sally didn't like it, I had to tell her the truth. In less than an hour she'd sacked me, packed as much of my stuff as she could in black plastic bags, and shouted, 'Get the filthy bitch out of my pub.' Dad was quiet while all this was going on; you see, what mum says goes. I didn't speak to them for months until I had to go back there because I needed some papers. They were cool, but fine. So I started seeing them again once or twice a week. After a while they lifted the ban on Sally coming to the pub. But then someone would say something in the pub and they'd get vicious again and tell me to go to the doctor and get some pills to cure me. One day Sally and I were watching *OUT*[2] on Channel 4. It was about parents of lesbians and gays and my mum rang and said, 'How do you think that makes me feel? I'll never be a grandmother through you.' I said, 'There's no law that says 'cos I'm a lesbian I can't have kids.' That's what put the thought in our minds really. When I told her I was pregnant she wanted to know how come. I just said, 'Pretty much the same as anyone else – little swimmers', and left it at that. I didn't want her to know we'd got a donor. She didn't come to see the baby for three weeks and when she did she was cold towards us again and said that Nerys was ugly, which really upset me. I'd had enough and told her, 'If we fall out now you'll never see us again. That's it, you're not gonna be up one day and down the next.' She's been fine since.

Daniel, 32, separated from his wife Bridget, 31, and two daughters Ruth, 6, and Mary, 4. *Aberdeen.*

Bridget and I met through mutual Christian friends. She knew I was gay before we met but she had never knowingly met a gay person, so our friends introduced us and we became friends. We were both going through a very zealous Christian phase and soon we felt God called us to be married. Now I see that my faith overrode my mental and practical faculties. I was unsure of my own feelings and so dogged obedience to God's calling was all I could do. She had romantic and spiritual feelings towards me. During the first two years of our marriage we had an active sex life which was very stressful for me, and then

Bridget became pregnant. Before Ruth was born we'd kept the lid on the marriage through both being very busy with work and church, and we didn't really need to face the massive contradictions in our marriage. Once Ruth was born, though, it brought all those issues to the surface. Having a child changes everything and our relationship wasn't firmly grounded enough to cope with it. We moved to a bigger flat in an area where Bridget knew no one, and I started a two-year course that meant I was only home in the evenings. This put the marriage into severe difficulty and we struggled on for two years, when our second child, Mary, was born. Bridget blamed our failing marriage on my sexuality, but I don't agree. It was bigger than that. I had no love or genuine feelings for her from the start, it was all duty; what is expected of us, what we were called to do by God. I have always defined myself as gay and I didn't allow myself to indulge those feelings. When Mary was one year old and Ruth three, Bridget and I separated. She now lives in a different flat with the kids in an area with good schools and I live in what was the family flat. I see the kids every other night and have them to stay on alternate weekends. I have to work overtime to make ends meet and pay for both flats and maintenance as Bridget hasn't had a job since the kids were born. It's hard going.

Kirk, 37, whose partner Keith, 43, is the natural father to Kelly, 15, and Stuart, 18. *Leeds*.

Keith was the first bisexual lover I'd had and when he told me, on our first night together, that his ex-wife and kids lived in the centre of town I just wanted to run for it. His wife had known that he was bisexual, but he had been going through a heterosexual phase and they had got married and had kids, with the sort of unspoken understanding that things might change again in the future. Anyway, Keith courted me for ages and wore me down and we eventually started living together, having his kids to stay for weekends and school holidays and contributing financially to them. When his ex-wife came with the kids to stay for Christmas for the first time she tried to stop us seeing them when they went home. I think she was worried after she saw that we could so obviously provide a loving and stable family environment while she was unable to keep them clean, clothed and fed, let alone the nicer things in life. We got our solicitor to issue a threatening letter about what would need to be aired if we challenged her for access and so she let us see the kids again regularly as before. After five years of this set-up, out of the blue, Keith's ex-wife phoned to say she couldn't cope on her own with the kids any more and that if we didn't take them, permanently, within two weeks she'd put them into care. Keith desperately wanted his kids and we knew they hadn't had a quality upbringing with their mother, quite the opposite. I didn't know what to do, I'd never wanted an instant family; but talking to lesbian mother friends of mine convinced me to give it a go. Keith and I collected the kids with their possessions in black bin bags and drove the two of them, smelly and dirty, all the way back to Leeds. We were living in a gay houseshare and there was no way we could live there with the kids, so the landlord agreed to 'chuck us out' so we could be emergency re-housed as homeless with kids. We got a small flat for a few weeks and then, just by chance, two weeks later the housing association we'd been registered with for two years, as a gay couple, offered us a flat. But it wasn't suitable now we had the kids. The housing association were brilliant though. Within less than two weeks they'd found us a three-bedroomed terraced house to live in. We're still there and the kids are now thriving young adults. I wouldn't have missed it for the world.

Norma, 42, and her partner Lesley, 28, co-parents to Josh, 6.
Bedfordshire.

We tried fostering; we got in touch with the authorities about it. A few weeks later a woman came round and asked us a lot of questions. She told us that we were the first lesbian couple in the whole area who had applied to foster, that it was a very long process and took a very long time and that at any point we could be turned down. We never heard another word from her. After that we applied to do the Link scheme, where you get trained by the social services and then you have a young disabled person, or a brother and sister as we did, and you take them out, visit each others' houses and so on. We knew the man that ran the scheme otherwise I don't think we'd have been taken on there either. It was very time-consuming, but we continued doing it until we had our own baby. We decided to go to a donor insemination clinic to be absolutely sure it was all safe for us and the baby. We're petrified of the risk of HIV especially, but there are so many genetic diseases that we felt we couldn't be too careful. We didn't realize it would be quite so expensive though. We were turned down by two clinics before we found one that would treat us as an openly lesbian couple. We didn't want to lie about our situation, we thought it could cause so many difficulties later, remembering what we'd said and so on. We did think of making a fuss about the clinics that turned us down, after all we are both professional women who are making a great job of bringing up Josh, but in the end we were just so relieved to have found a helpful clinic.

Billie, 38, who co-parents her son Jamie, 7, with her partner Simone, 36, the donor father Mike, 36, and his partner Mehmet, 31. *London.*

Mike and I had been friends for years and he was the ideal man to be the donor father for the child that me and Simone had decided for a long time we wanted. Mike's lover, Mehmet, comes from a large family and it was him that convinced us that the four of us could do a great job of bringing up the child. It's all just been so civilized and happy. Jamie lives with me and Simone, but stays with Mike and Mehmet often, and with four of us to look after Jamie, plus umpteen friends who view Jamie as their surrogate son, we have a foolproof support network for us and him and he couldn't be more loved.

Mark, 40, and Hassan, 31, have been carers to three Albert Kennedy Trust (AKT) teenagers. *London.*

We chose not to have our own children, so it seemed natural to care for other people's cast-offs and rejects that they can't handle. It wasn't a parental drive that made us want to do this. Also, they're teenagers, they're with you for a year or so and they're off; so 'Oh I want a baby' is not an appropriate perspective or desire for becoming an Albert Kennedy Trust parent or carer. We wanted to fix things that we thought were outrageous. You just can't help but be moved by some of these kids' stories. We could have been fathers ourselves, there are many ways for gay men to achieve that. But we don't equate that with being AKT carers. This isn't a replacement for a romantic notion of having our own kids. We want to help young people with their lives, and help them to set themselves up. We have recently gained approval as foster carers with our local authority. When we first applied they asked us if we wanted to adopt or foster. We had to think long and hard about that; did we want to adopt a one-year-old child? For us that seemed strangely possessive, almost a selfish act in many respects. It felt like we were looking for something to own by adopting a child. We think being Albert Kennedy Trust carers is the best role for us.[3]

Gareth, 37, donor father to three daughters – Sasha, 3, Ella, 2, and Alicia, 1 – by different mothers. *Surrey.*

I have three daughters by three different women, all of whom are bringing up the kids with their female partners. I came from a very stable working-class background in Wales and had a secure loving background. I realize what a great start that gave me in life and I always thought I'd have children of my own to give them an equally good start. But I never knew how I'd go about that. With my first daughter I know very little about the set up between the mother and her partner. I did that as a blind AID (artificial insemination by donor) on the basis that I would be disclosed to the child, so he or she would have a name and know who their father was. I'd been attending a gay and lesbian parenting group that set up a register of gay men who were willing to donate to lesbian women. Sort of a lesbian insemination unit really. All the mothers of my daughters contacted me through this group. I was contacted by friends of the couple who were to be the mothers of my first daughter. They said they just wanted a donor father but wanted to retain the right to inform the child who the father was, should he or she ask. I have been given a picture of her, and her mother and partner wrote to me to thank me for my involvement, but I had no further contact and don't know where they live or what they do. I do believe she is in a secure environment. One thing I did find out by accident from one of the 'runners' who came to collect my donation was that the baby would be brought up in a Jewish household; which is fine by me, even though I'm a Welsh Baptist originally. I was quite hurt in the end that I was not even to have basic details of my daughter, so for my second and third daughters I made sure that I would get some sort of access and contact with the child. However, I don't think anything you embark on of this nature is ever going to turn out as you expect. With my second and third daughters I do have contact with their mothers and partners. They are both middle-class couples, living a very stable lower-middle-class life, professional women, property owners. The mother of my second daughter is estranged from her family – I'm not sure if that's to do with her sexuality. My third daughter has a large extended family of both sets of grandparents and they all think the world of her, which is great. The mothers of my second daughter are only now coming to realize that I am not a threat to the child or their custody. At the beginning they found my contact and involvement intrusive, but they now see me in a more positive light. I can see my youngest daughter as and when I want. We agreed once a month but if I'm in the area I can drop in and there's no problem about that. With my middle daughter the arrangement was four visits a year plus Christmas and birthday, but in reality I see her more often, although I do have to check it is convenient to everyone. My younger two daughters are going to know me as their father. I would like more access to my daughters but these things will evolve into less-formal arrangements, I'm sure, in time. But basically I am happy with the contact I have with my younger daughters. I do have a partner at the moment, but I didn't at the time of making the donations. It was very important to me to father children with lesbian couples. I wouldn't have been interested in co-parenting with a heterosexual mother. There would have been too many doubts in my mind as to whether, at a future date, my sexuality could be used against me to deny contact with the children. Having children has made me calm down in my life and not keep looking around for something that was missing. The fulfilment that having children has given me has made me more able to conduct a stable relationship. I feel as if I'm not searching for something desperately any more. I'm much calmer about the life to come and how my life will unfold.

Simon, 38, and his lover Giles, 43, with Nita, 37, and Cheryl, 39, are co-parents to James, 8, and Edward, 6. *Kent.*

I came to be a father as a result of a request that was made many years ago by a very close friend of mine. Cheryl is a lesbian and she and her partner approached me and my partner because we were all very close to the idea of being co-parents. When they split up we all forgot about it, but when Cheryl teamed up with someone else and they were settled, they revived the idea, and that's how it came about some years later. We knew both of them even before they got together, and when their body-clocks got to the point where they had to make a decision about whether they wanted to have children or not . . . they asked us. They were both living with us when they broached the subject again. Cheryl, who decided to become the mother, was initially married and broke up with her husband. So she came to live with us for a while. Her new partner also came to live with us, for several months. That describes the closeness of the relationship between the four of us. For that reason we didn't really discuss how things would be once the kids were born. Things like how much involvement my partner and I would have and so on. We just all knew I would be the donor father and that the kids would live with the two women in their home, and Giles and I would be around to help out financially and practically, as and when we could. As we were all so close it may be a little more understandable that we didn't discuss those sorts of things. And the other thing is that we are all pretty feather-brained about things like that, I think. It's true to say that we do things first and then think afterwards. It's not the best way of going about things, but, fortunately, in this case it has worked out all right. Nita also wanted a child and two years later she decided, being black, that she wanted a black donor father. So our second son is a sperm-bank baby, we have no contact with the natural father, and we all accept him as our son. He calls me 'daddy' even though he knows the full situation and I think of him very much as my son too.

Sandra, 29, mother to Amani, 3, whom she co-parents with Danny, 34. London.

None of my family knows I'm a lesbian. A few of my friends do but most of my friends don't have a clue about my sexuality. I wanted a child, and I was with my partner for over three years when we decided to go for it. She's black too and we wanted a black donor father. I have very few gay or lesbian friends, but one of my best friends, Danny, is gay and was more than happy to be the donor father. Initially my girlfriend and I weren't going to share the parenting with him, but when she left me less than a year after the baby was born I needed help, and Danny was the obvious person. Now Danny and I share a flat, separate bedrooms of course, and are bringing up Amani together. It's working fine. I tell my family we are just friends and don't sleep together but they just say, 'Yes, Sandra, of course you don't.' They know he's the father and so it all fits a nice cosy pattern for them. I don't know if it is a particular issue for the black community or whether white lesbians have as much hostility from the white community, but I'm certainly not about to come out to everyone and expect to be treated the same. Of course there are loads of black people who aren't homophobic at all, but they're certainly not members of my family.

Belinda, 36, and Jane, 34, mothers to Alice, 2. *London.*

We're two mummies and a baby. That's how we see ourselves. We don't see Alice's father as a part of our nuclear family. Our extended family includes my parents and grandmother, Jane's brother, but not Jane's parents. Jane's mother is unhappy about the situation, but that's part and parcel of her being unhappy about Jane's sexuality anyway. Having Alice has only fuelled that antagonism. When Jane told her that I was having a baby she initially thought 'Brilliant!', that Jane'd been let off the hook because I'd found myself a boyfriend. When Jane explained we were going to bring up the baby together she was very unhappy. We told her six months before the baby was born and it wasn't until three months after the birth that she rang up to see how I was or even alluded to my existence. Her father is very old and I don't think that he is aware of the circumstances anyway. It's her mother who is very difficult about it. Jane describes herself as coming from very bigoted Northern Irish Presbyterian stock and they find it all very alien. Her mother condemns many different sections of society, so it's not just us, but it's unfortunate because she's missing out on Alice and lots of other happy stuff. But she can't stop seeing it as Jane wasting her life. It's not just to do with sexuality though. She's very disapproving of Jane's brother and his wife too. She doesn't see Alice as her granddaughter; 'It's Belinda's baby, what has that got to do with me?' is how she feels. My parents on the other hand, ever since she was born, have been very, very fond of Alice. It hasn't always been like that though. My father found it difficult to come to terms with me having a baby at first. He once told me that I had no right to even consider having a baby. But since she's been born and he can see that we can support her in what he would consider an admirable fashion, he's been fine about it. My grandmother was the one who never batted an eyelid, she does sometimes ask if we've seen Gary recently, that's Alice's father, but she dotes on Alice and on Jane as well. My family views Jane very much as the adopted daughter.

Graham, 47, father to Yvonne, 27. *London and Yorkshire.*

I was the seventeenth child of seventeen children and my mother said that she realized after fifteen that the safe period wasn't in the middle of the month. I'm quite fond of children. I've got a very, very big family, as you can imagine. There's sixty nieces and nephews, and twenty great-nieces and nephews. Growing up in Yorkshire we thought that we were left on the shelf if we weren't married by the time we were nineteen or twenty. It was regarded as a little bit odd. I was nineteen when I got married because I thought that there was something wrong with me. I was a bit of a loner at school, and when a woman came along and showed a bit of interest – I'd never had a girlfriend or a boyfriend – I lapped it up, of course. It caused a lot of problems eventually, because I hadn't come to terms with myself. Having a child I think was an attempt to save our marriage and I've got a very nice daughter.

I think that she (my wife) was the first person to show me outside my family that somebody could be caring and say 'I love you', which was very unusual for me, and I couldn't believe somebody was saying it. It didn't last very long, because there was a spectre looming. About three weeks after we got married I started an affair with a married man. My wife and I very nearly split up, but we tried everything possible to stay together, and I think having the child was one of them. The marriage lasted officially three years, that's up to divorce. But we separated after two and a half years, when my daughter was about fifteen months old. We split up fairly amicably but then I went away to university and to live abroad. I just kept in contact with letters and presents from abroad mainly, and a visit a couple of times a year maybe. I didn't really have a lot of contact with her, until she was thirteen and I was living with my present partner, whom I've been with for fifteen years now. So she was brought along to visit us in our gay household when she was thirteen. I think she coped very well with it.

She was very difficult as well, but I don't know if that was because she had sussed out that there was something going on between me and my partner. She thought that she'd been neglected. She never wants to discuss it really. I'm very open about my gay relationship. I didn't necessarily take her aside and say 'this is the situation'. I thought it was best for her to ask the questions and for me to answer them, rather than to force anything on her.

John, now divorced, father to Gary, 11, and Emma, 10. *Hull.*

I was married for ten years and then divorced. The marriage ended when my wife went off with what was supposedly my best friend about six years ago now. I have two children; my ex-wife has custody of them and has re-married. I have access and I live with my partner, Tom, so the kids come to stay with me for weekends.

I'm not sure if my wife has any idea or inkling of the real situation that I'm living in at the moment. I don't particularly think that it is any of her business, and I'm sure that if she did know she would cause trouble because our relations are not brilliant, so I keep it to myself. And as far as she's aware, she knows I'm living in another house with another man, but just as friends basically.

I don't think she would have much suspicion as to my real sexuality because sex between us wasn't any problem. It was regular, I don't know, once a week I suppose, or something like that, for a period of ten years, and I never, during that period, went with a man. Although I was attracted to them, I never did. I was never unfaithful with either a man or a woman. Men just didn't enter into the equation at that particular time.

If you had said I'd end up living with another man, I'd have thought you'd gone mad. I'm glad it has turned out like this, because otherwise it would have got more and more frustrated, the gay bit inside me. It always surfaces, and then if you're married you push it down again, but it keeps coming back up, and ultimately it's always there. I'm fairly traditional and when we first started out I thought that I'd stay married to her until I die. If she hadn't gone off, I still would have been. I would have pushed it down, and pushed it down, and sort of denied my gay side. I've got the ability to do that, I'm fairly sort of strong-willed, and it wouldn't have arisen.

If I could press a button and be straight then I would. No question of that, I would. I'm not ashamed of being gay, although obviously that conflicts to some extent with what I've just said. I suppose, I'm a hypocrite on that one, I'm not sure. It's simply a question of having an easier life. Why make life more difficult by questions of sexuality? I can't say I was so proud of being straight when I was living a straight lifestyle. So why should I be proud, living a gay lifestyle?

Pam, 40, now separated from Rhona, 25, and their son, Nicky, 6.
Bristol.

When I met Rhona she already had Nicky, he was one year old. She had been living with a man and it was his child, but he wanted nothing to do with parenting. Rhona's mother was looking after Nicky because she couldn't cope on her own. When Rhona and I set up home together Nicky came to live with us, but it was without discussion or planning. He was with us one weekend and Rhona said, 'He might as well stay, eh?' We got a house on quite a rough estate and after a while we started getting abuse and trouble from some of the local lads. But we lived there for nearly three years together, putting up with the occasional nastiness. One day Rhona came home to find the place being burgled, but they didn't run off when she came in; they stayed and sexually assaulted her. We can't help feeling it was because they didn't like the fact that Rhona and I were bringing up a child without anyone like them around. With attitudes and behaviour like theirs it's hardly surprising no one wants them. And neither did we. After Rhona was attacked in our own home, we moved within a few days. We went to live in the country with my parents for a while, but unfortunately a few months later we split up. Rhona and Nicky live about thirty miles away now and I see Nicky often. She's living with another man and I'm really worried that sooner or later they'll move away or they'll decide it's best if I don't see Nicky any more. I have no rights at all but I still feel very much his parent.

Gwen, 59, grandmother to Max, 1, and mother to Wendy, 30.
Liverpool.

My partner and I were the only lesbian parents living together that we knew, for many years. We had single lesbian friends with kids, we knew married women with kids who managed to live with their husbands and have a secret lesbian life for a small part of the time, and we knew closeted lesbian couples who lived together but had no kids. We, however, felt like real pioneers as overt lesbians (not as out as younger people today are, but in the mid-1960s and early 1970s we're still talking about a pretty radical lifestyle) with a child we were bringing up together. My only regret is that the child was the result of a fit of conformity (yes, I had a fling with a man!) that I indulged in before I accepted myself. It would have been great to have conceived via a donor father, but it wasn't something we really knew about then. Sadly, my partner, who was quite a bit older than me, died a few years ago, but I'm determined not to let her down, so I'm living life to the full. I have big plans for my grandson; my daughter, however, is a lost cause, I fear. She is happily married, respectable and frightfully conformist; a reaction to me and her upbringing maybe? Ooh, what challenges lie ahead!

Notes

1. *Spare Rib*, Radical feminist magazine of the 1970s, 1980s and early 1990s, no longer being published.
2. *OUT*, the UK's first regular lesbian and gay magazine programme on Channel 4 television, started in 1989 and ran through the early 1990s. No longer made, but regular lesbian and gay programming on Channel 4, BBC2 and BBC Radio 5 was created in its wake.
3. See Chapter 15 for further details and case histories from the Albert Kennedy Trust.

TWO

Why Bother?

There are many reasons for lesbians and gay men wanting to become parents, and the myriad routes to parenthood complicate the reasoning further. Those who were in heterosexual marriages when their children were born have more expected reasons for becoming parents.

Glenda, 31, who co-parents with Sally, 40, their daughter Nerys, 4.
Southampton.

I never wanted children, but when Sally started talking about having a baby I really got into it and I really wanted one then. But I wasn't maternal, it didn't mean that much to me, not until she left my body and then you can't explain the overwhelming bond; you would do anything for them. Some people say there are too many people in the world already; well, then, a few more won't matter. Stop the heterosexuals having them – let us have a go instead. Kids are taken for granted often in a straight family, but with a gay family I think you're more aware of what's going on and more determined to make a good job of it because of all the thinking and planning you have to do to get a kid. We didn't have to have a child; as a lesbian couple we don't have that expectation on us, but it's everyone's right and I knew we could do a bloody good job of being parents, so why not? As long as the authorities don't go poking their noses in.

Daniel, 32, separated from his wife, Bridget, 31, and two daughters Ruth, 6, and Mary, 4. *Aberdeen.*

We had talked about having kids and I was so curious to know what my kids would be like. I think everyone imagines that. Being in a Christian marriage it was our duty sooner or later to have kids. So it was when, rather than if or why, we would have children. We didn't admit to ourselves, maybe even didn't realize, that it was not the right situation for having kids. It was our duty, if the marriage is working, to have kids. It would have meant acknowledging a lack of happiness and belief in our faith and in our duty as a married couple. I also thought that having kids would distract me from the pain of the marriage and help lessen the contradiction of being a gay man in a straight marriage. It didn't. In fact, it did the opposite.

John, now divorced, father to Gary, 11, and Emma, 10. *Hull.*

I got married probably because it was the done thing to do. I mean I come from a northern background, we were a very traditional sort of family. You couldn't be gay really. I mean I suppose I was. Although I suppose people would label me as bisexual, because I could quite easily have sex with a man or a woman. And it was just the thing to do. And I did love my wife at the time, no question about that, so we got married.

I wanted to have children, rather for the same reason as I got married, I suppose. Because it was the done thing. Although the first one wasn't exactly planned, he just occurred, the second most definitely was planned. Because again I thought I was in a marriage for good and children were going to be part of it. It was just part of the picture that I was expected to paint I suppose. And I just decided to go along with it. Children come with marriage and that was it and once you've got obligations you have to see it through, even though we've split up.

When it comes to same-sex couples who are having the baby outside of a heterosexual marriage, the reasons for wanting kids become more diverse.

Samantha, 39, mother to two adult daughters, 19 and 23, and co-parent, with her lover Stella, 28, to Holly, 2. *Kent.*

I kept telling Stella that having a child is something that every woman should do, an experience not to be missed. Also, I couldn't have any more kids and Stella was quite happy to have the baby. The other reason was that I had had a living hell of a marriage – violent, abusive – and being with Stella is so different, so calm and loving, that I knew it would be such a happy, loving environment to bring a child up in.

Gareth, 37, donor father to three daughters – Sasha, 3, Ella, 2, and Alicia, 1 – by different mothers. *Surrey*.

Being a gay man shouldn't be a bar to being a father. It took me some time to see that it wasn't a disqualification. A lot of gay men have been fathers in the past. A lot of arrangements like this have occurred in the past. I know a number of older gay men who are now grandfathers from arrangements with lesbian couples in the 1950s and 1960s. As a man with no religious beliefs, I did want a part of me to go on. I felt my own childhood had been happy and secure and I wanted other people to have a similar experience to me. A lot of gay men and lesbians will tell you they had very unhappy family lives.[1] Most of them have very negative attitudes to family life. I'm very involved with my extended family and my close family and I enjoy that very much. A lot of women say that deep down they have strong maternal urges that lead them towards motherhood, whether they are straight or lesbian. For some men, straight or gay, the same sort of deep-rooted, burning paternalism is present.[2] I felt I would always have children, it was a question of getting over in my own mind that being gay wasn't a disqualification. As a father I have a sense of fulfilment and completeness. You get something you can't get from a relationship with another adult; there is someone who looks like you or like relatives of yours. It's something very fulfilling and probably incapable of expression. . . it's called parenthood. The world is over-populated and people might legitimately say, 'Why are you bringing even more children into the world?' But there are a lot of gay men who aren't going to have children, so I'm having a few for them to keep the population at replacement level. Also, I don't know what proportion of children are the result of accidents or women just not having access to contraception, but all of my children have been desperately wanted, very much loved and excellently cared for. Perhaps we should be questioning bringing kids into situations where they are not going to have any of these things. I have no qualms about having helped bring three more children onto the face of the earth. Whether it will be the sort of earth that I've enjoyed, I don't know; who does?

Simon, 38, and his lover Giles, 43, with Nita, 37, and Cheryl, 39, are co-parents to James, 8, and Edward, 6. *Kent.*

Nothing appealed to me about becoming a father at all. I had no interest in children. . . well that's not quite true, but I had no interest in becoming a father. The idea was really to oblige our friends. We were by this stage, all four of us, in a close relationship. We saw a lot of each other; Cheryl came to live with us for a few months when her marriage broke up and both she and Nita lived with us for a while too. So once they were settled in their own place it seemed the appropriate environment into which to bring a child, and I had no objection to it. It's only since the children have come along, that I've actually grown into the role of being a father quite happily.

Belinda, 36, and Jane, 34, mothers to Alice, 2. *London.*

I wanted a family. A family is important to me. I felt unfulfilled, even though I'd been with Jane for years. I saw having a child as the most creative thing one can do. I wouldn't have continued trying for five years and pumped nasty chemicals into my body and had an operation if it wasn't something I really wanted to do. I know it seems that as a lesbian I don't have the automatic expectation on me of being a mother; and in the mid-1980s I wouldn't have thought this way. At college I read all those books and agreed that we as lesbians should withhold our bodies from the service of the patriarchal society; radical lesbian feminism – nothing to do with men at all. Then I did dabble with married men for a while too, I don't know why! But by my mid-twenties I knew I wanted to have a child and by the time I was thirty decided to do something about it.

Graham, 47, father to Yvonne, 27. *London and Yorkshire.*

If I had had a gay relationship earlier on in life I would never have got married and I certainly wouldn't have wanted children. There's no particular need to have children. I've got an unbelievable number of nieces and nephews, I was a great-uncle when I was twenty-one, I was an uncle before I was born. I'm more conscious about the population issue in the world. The planet is dying because there are too many people in the world. I think that I might have been aware of over-population even twenty years ago, and that might have had some bearing on it too. But the main thing was that. . . it's not the be-all and end-all to have children, is it.

I don't know why a lot of homosexual people want to have kids. But then there are a lot of things about my life that people maybe don't understand. I do get a little bemused by it. I hope it's not the kitten mentality. You know, it's nice to have a little kitten for Christmas, wouldn't it be nice to have a nice little child? There are the realities of a kid bawling its eyes out for weeks on end with teething problems, and all the other things to do with parenthood, which have to do with you being selfless and self-effacing at times. So I don't know why lesbian and gay people do it; we can avoid it, we don't have the automatic expectation of reproducing, in our different sexuality, why would you want to?

I think that it is interesting to think that you can produce another living being. I don't know if that's what people want to do. You can't believe that you can actually do it, and that there's another living entity that is part of you, and part of another person, of course. But I still don't think that I would have done it. There's no real reason why one should have wanted to necessarily do it.

Maggie, 36, and Shelley, 40, mothers to twins, 4. *London.*

Maggie: I suppose lesbians have a whole range of reasons for having kids.[3] I certainly did. I enjoy looking after children, I always have done. Also I suppose I realized that you are put on this earth for a very short space of time in reality and you can't do very much in it. And I thought maybe I could have my chance at influencing the world after I had gone by producing a child who was going to carry things on, or at least be a sane human being if they were brought up in a relatively nice environment and were cherished, wanted, loved and helped to think, and maybe they would be a nice person too. I wasn't expecting too much, I must say. But I think I thought that there is very little in this world of any significance apart from what goes on after you've died really. And I wasn't expecting to be a great revolutionary or do anything really dramatic in my life that I'd become famous for. And I thought, what's it all for, why not have children? And it seemed as good a way as any, to pass the time.

I'd say I had loads of regrets, very early on, because it was real hell. A relationship breaking up, two small babies, a lot of hostility, a lot of resentment from people at work. It was really very, very hard. I'd say now that it's only beginning to feel like it was a nice thing to do. They really are a lot of fun at the moment. And I'm enjoying it much more than I ever did. It depends on when you ask, I suspect, and what time of day you ask, and how well they are behaving lately. I am enjoying it a lot now, I certainly didn't at first. I hated it. Small babies could be the death of anybody I expect. A lot of hard, shit work.

Shelley: No. I didn't want children. I've been told at this point, by Maggie, to confess that I was at one point married. The relationship lasted for about ten years and during that relationship I had decided that I wasn't so desperate to have children that it ever became a good idea. It seemed to me that it was more important to have a relationship that worked well, before anyone decided to have children. Given that that relationship was doomed to failure because he was male, we'd never got round to it. I went on to another relationship with another man, and the longer time went on, the more I thought I'm never going to get to the point where it's a good idea to have children, therefore I should just accept that I'm not desperate to have children. I don't have any of the maternal instincts that everyone tells me that I should have in order to have children. So I didn't do it. At the same time I enjoy being with children, I enjoy playing with them, and I even trained as a teacher and did all sorts of things around kids. It wasn't a decision that I didn't want to have anything to do with children, it was just that I didn't want to produce any of my own. In fact, I did think, strangely, like some people do, that at some point in the distant future, when I was more settled, I might foster children, perhaps who were difficult to place. But then I met Maggie who already had two children that we couldn't send back. So it was a decision that I had to make about the relationship that I wanted to have with Maggie, whether I could accept that that relationship was with Maggie and two children, and whether that was going to be good, as far as I was concerned. And clearly I decided it was, otherwise I wouldn't be here.

What I didn't ever really want to be was at the leading edge of social change. I mean, I happen to be a lesbian, I didn't choose that, I am one. And I happen to be part of a family with two small children. I didn't actually choose that, except in a sense that Maggie and the children existed when I met her, and I wanted to be with all of them. But if I'd been asked earlier than that, I wouldn't have actively chosen to have a family with children in it. But being here with my family of Maggie and the twins is a very definite choice of mine and where I prefer to be.

Pam, 40, now separated from Rhona, 25, and their son, Nicky, 6. *Bristol.*

I really wanted to be a parent, for a long time. When I met Rhona she already had Nicky and we just wanted to be together. We co-parented him for over three years and we were very much both his mothers. In fact you could say I was the more nurturing of the two of us. We have split up since and Rhona is living with a man again, who is now seen as Nicky's stepfather. I am desperately worried that they will move away or lessen the contact I have with him. I want to continue being his parent; even though I'm not his natural mother I still feel I am one of his parents and he thinks so too. It's getting late for me to have my own child, I'm forty now, and I'd want to have it on my own.[4] I have become very wary of co-parenting, especially when you are not the natural mother. But I've got so much to give, I definitely want to be a parent and intend to continue being Nicky's parent too.

Jim, 38, single father to Hayley, 8, born to a surrogate mother. *Isle of Wight.*

It was in my heart that I wanted to be a father. I was living with Jack, we'd been together for five years, and the subject of children kept coming up, it was always there. He'd had two children from a previous marriage and he'd decided that he didn't want to have any contact with them. I think this was out of fear. He was afraid of his ex-wife's family; big East End family, very hard, very macho, he was afraid of how they would react if they knew he was gay. He didn't want his own family to find out either. But within two years of us being together he went back to his mum's after we had a row and told her he was gay. She wouldn't have this. She said it was because he'd moved in with me and it was my influence and he should move out as quickly as possible and he'll be saved. But we ended up staying together for another ten years before he eventually left, so it was twelve years altogether. Five years into that relationship we decided to go ahead and have a child of our own. Initially this came from myself. It was something that I'd wanted. It was the one big regret that I had about being gay. I couldn't accept that being gay should prohibit me from having a child. So I started the ball rolling and I kept on about it. Eventually he decided that it would be a good idea. He wanted it as much as I did. We talked long and hard about it. It wasn't a light decision. Although, having said that, I did have some illusions about what it would be like. I was pretty naive about what having children meant at that point. Of course Jack wasn't, he'd had two children. I didn't realize the impact that it would have on my lifestyle and all that. I only knew that I wanted a child. I wanted to put right something that had gone wrong in my own childhood. Basically I had an evil childhood. A wicked stepmother and a very abusive father; physical, mental and sexual abuse. All that sort of stuff. It took me a long time to get over that, many years. I had to do something about it, but there was nothing that I could do to get over it, except have a child of my own. I did consider working with kids in care or something like that but there was also the problem I had with being gay. That worried me, that frightened me, and I didn't come to terms with that until I was twenty-four. I thought that being gay would damage me professionally and I thought that it would get back to my employers that I was gay and working with children, and they wouldn't want that, because of all the old myths about us being unfit to be in charge of kids. So I ruled it out, it just wasn't possible I thought. So fatherhood seemed to be the logical answer at the time and as things have worked out, it was a good thing.

Notes

1. A.M. Boxer, J.A. Cook and G. Herdt (1991) Identity transitions and parent-child relations among gay and lesbian youth. In K. Pillemer and K. McCartney (eds), *Parent–Child Relations Throughout Life*. Hillsdale, NJ: Erlbaum.

2. J.J. Bigner and R.B. Jacobsen (1989) Parenting behaviours of homosexual and heterosexual fathers. *Journal of Homosexuality*, 18: 173–86.

3. Cheri Pies (1985) *Considering Parenthood: A Workbook for Lesbians*. San Francisco: Spinsters/Aunt Lute.

4. R. Lesser (1991) Deciding not to become a mother. In B. Sang, J. Warshow and A. Smith (eds), *Lesbians at Midlife*. San Francisco: The Spinsters Book Co., pp. 84–90.

THREE

Negotiating Parenthood

In a heterosexual marriage there are many automatic assumptions, roles and legal conditions that apply when a couple have a child together. For same-sex couples and other lesbian and gay parenting arrangements it is a very different picture. So parenthood has to be negotiated, to greater or lesser degrees.

Belinda, 36, and Jane, 34, mothers to Alice, 2. *London*.

We'd found out that whatever parenting agreement we drew up, it wouldn't actually be legally binding. So we decided to agree face to face what we all wanted and expected out of having a child between us. Gary then sent us a letter setting out what we'd all agreed in black and white and that was the basis on which we all proceeded. We decided Gary would have no financial involvement; that was probably the main thing, our independence as lesbian mothers, but we wanted Alice to know that he is her natural father. We wouldn't necessarily have encouraged her to call him daddy, but it seems to have happened because he has taught Alice to call him that, which we've found difficult to counteract. It's OK if we stick to him seeing Alice only every few weeks, even though originally we said every other month. Alice may well decide at fourteen that we can go and get stuffed and she's going to live with him; she has a right to make those decisions. But at the outset we were all three very keen to stress that Jane and I would be the people who would parent Alice and he would be there in the background. We haven't discouraged him or forgotten about him, quite the opposite. We think it's a much better arrangement than we would have had if I'd become pregnant through a sperm bank. So we are happy with the arrangement and it has worked out quite well really, we're very comfortable with Gary. We all have a very good understanding.

Glenda, 31, who co-parents with Sally, 40, their daughter Nerys, 4.
Southampton.

We decided that I would have the baby because Sally has thyroid trouble and was very ill with her last baby when she was married. That was the only agreement between the two of us really. We realize that as the natural mother, I would have more rights to our daughter than Sally, but we couldn't do anything about that before the baby was born. Finding a donor was the tricky bit. We didn't really know how to go about it, but we knew what agreements we wanted. We wanted just his sperm, no contact afterwards, nothing. This was going to be *our*, mine and Sally's, baby. There wasn't a great list of donors to choose from. It was word of mouth through friends who knew we wanted a baby, not a husband, and someone came along. He was happy with what we wanted. He didn't want any contact with the baby afterwards. He was just happy to be the donor and wanted to know that he could do it and that his genes were being passed on somewhere. He was a roaming friend of a friend. Never in one place very long. He didn't want a baby to take care of. We wanted to make sure he was medically sound and hadn't got AIDS or anything else that could harm us or the baby, but we didn't really have the facilities or the know-how to check up.[1] We took his word for it that he was clean. He was definitely straight. I don't know if he was promiscuous. It was a dangerous thing to do, but at the time it was our only choice. He was the only one offering us what we wanted and he was happy to agree to our requests; for him it was like having a haircut, for us it was a massive problem. We've been lucky; we've got a healthy two-year-old.

Some people recommend drawing up agreements between the natural parents before the child is conceived or born; either to safeguard the rights of access to the child, or to avoid contact, or to ensure the parenting rights of the same-sex partners involved or to guarantee the guardianship of the child should anything happen to the natural mother or father. In practice, however, it is not possible to guarantee any of these by prior arrangement. In the UK the courts will always make up their own minds about what is in the best interests of the child concerned. This doesn't stop agreements being drawn up, but they should be viewed as agreements of honour rather than legally binding documents.[2]

Gareth, 37, donor father to three daughters – Sasha, 3, Ella, 2, and Alicia, 1 – by different mothers. *Surrey*.

Before I started donating, particularly with the mothers of my younger two daughters, I wrote them a letter stating the terms on which I'd like to proceed. Most of it was to do with the detail of how I was to make the donation, but a lot of it was also to explain that I didn't want to proceed unless I could see the child. So I spelled out the sort of access and involvement I would have with the child. I only have a photo and the birth date of my first daughter. That is all I know about her, which took me a long time to come to terms with; I was very hurt by that behaviour. So when I decided to father another child, I wanted to make quite sure that I would have some sort of access to the child and that the parents were quite aware of that intention before we started. Although I couldn't offer to share in the child's upbringing, I did want to see the child regularly and that he or she would know that I am their father. I suppose deep down I would have liked to have a child I could bring up. But you have to realize the limitations and impracticalities of that sort of thing. I'm a professional man holding down a very stressful job; for me to bring up a child would have been impractical unless I was able to provide nannies almost non-stop. As a lawyer, I'm not sure whether these sort of arrangements are enforceable by the courts. I doubt it. If at some future point access was withdrawn, I suspect a court would restore it to the level at which access was being given previously; as long as the visiting parent cannot be shown to be a danger to the children or to exert any untoward influence over them. In any event, in all parenting decisions you need to take one step at a time; parenting isn't easy. Were there to be any disputes, the courts would look at the interests of the child (which they would always regard as paramount) and the continuity of parenthood (especially for older children), irrespective of what either of the parents thinks.[3] This contrasts with the attitude in the USA, where the rights to children are considered rather like chattels or personal effects to be fought over. Simple disputes over access being denied should not be difficult to resolve. The courts would look at what the past arrangements had been and probably restore those. For lesbian women it is important to get a gay man as a parent to father a child, because many of them have this fear that their children will be taken away just because they are lesbian. The fact that the father is gay neutralizes this sexuality problem. In my opinion, though, this is a fear about something that is not necessarily present. If lesbians have had children taken away from them you'd probably find there were other much more serious factors as to why the children were taken away, rather than just one's sexuality. I've only known one case like that and in that case the lesbian mother was a heroin addict. She was adamant that her losing custody was because of her sexuality. I think the court was rather disturbed that a child was being brought up in what was basically a smack house. An extreme example, I know, but it illustrates my point.

The mothers of my second and third daughters, and their partners, responded to my letters of agreement saying they had no problem with my proposals. They all thought that putting things down in black and white was helpful and therefore we all knew what we were entering into. In practice we have all strayed outside the strict terms of that letter, but as a parent you have to be flexible and one never knows how it's going to develop. I'm actually having more access to both of my younger daughters than was initially proposed.

Simon, 38, and his lover Giles, 43, with Nita, 37, and Cheryl, 39, are co-parents to James, 8, and Edward, 6. Kent.

To tell you the truth, we went into it in the best way possible. I've heard since that people really ought to make things clear about what the terms and conditions are. In our case we didn't make any such things clear at all. The nature of our relationship was such that we were very casual about things. When they asked me to be a father, they didn't put any conditions forward, nor did we. They did not even, and I think perhaps this was rather foolhardy, ask for an HIV test. On the other hand, they had known that my partner and I had been in a relationship for many years, but then you can't trust that at all. They also knew that my own habits were, well, unexciting to say the least, simply because that's the way I am.

Kirk, 37, whose partner Keith, 43, is the natural father to Kelly, 15, and Stuart, 18. Leeds.

There was nothing to negotiate; it was all or nothing. Keith's ex-wife had not been coping with their two kids as a single parent. Stuart, who was ten at the time, had been looking after his younger sister for years already when he moved in with us. From his school diary work we saw that he had had to be responsible for getting his sister up, feeding her, making packed lunches and taking her to and from school. After school he would either get their tea or both of them would go down to the market where their mother worked and wait, sometimes until ten at night, when they would get chips and cocoa and then go home to bed. It's not that their mother wasn't working hard, far from it, but she just wasn't able to care adequately for them. Keith's parents set her up in the business venture and when she went bankrupt it was the final straw. There had been a reconciliation between Keith and his parents and I think they also saw in me a stable family environment in the making, especially as I'm an ex-teacher, so I'm sure they put pressure on to force the change. The only choice I had was, do I stay with Keith and become the co-parent of his kids or do I leave? I stayed.

Many more decisions were made for us too. There was no time or opportunity to plan and choose the best time to become parents. We had fourteen days' notice and we were both working full-time. Keith had to give up his job, they wouldn't let him go part-time because he was a union activist and they were looking for any reason to get rid of him. We couldn't stay in our gay houseshare because there wasn't enough room and the other guys there wouldn't put up with kids around the house anyway. So we got the landlord to agree to kick us out so we could apply for, and we got, emergency housing and then luckily a housing association house. The association was very gay-friendly and our solicitor happened to be one of the board of management and she was very pro-gay, so it actually was an advantage being a gay couple in this case. I don't think we'd have got a place so quickly without all these factors.

So within a few weeks we went from two full-time working men in a fun-loving gay relationship, to a one-wage four-person household including two kids to care for. Keith was pretty rusty as a parent and although I'd been a teacher it's a very different ball game to having kids in your own house. You don't have time to sit down and negotiate parenthood in a situation like that. You just get on with it.

Maggie, 36, and Shelley, 40, mothers to twins, 4. *London*.

Shelley: I was attracted to Maggie and I wanted to have a relationship with her, but I was clear from the start that that meant a relationship with three people, not just with one. Two of them quite small at the time, six months old, but nevertheless three people. And it certainly wouldn't ever have been something I would have chosen to do; if anyone had ever asked something about having children, I would have said no. Not that I don't love kids, and I've had lots to do with kids over the years. But I like them to play with and to talk to, and then to pass back to their parents. That would be my favourite way of dealing with it. But there you are; the relationship was important and I thought, despite my reservations, I'd probably make a reasonable go of being a mother. It's not work in progress. Who knows what's round the next corner, and who knows what tomorrow brings, but as far as one is able to say, I think that we've got a lifelong relationship here. That would be my view. And we talked a lot before we started living together about what would happen if we started a permanent living-together relationship and that didn't succeed, what would happen in respect of the children, because I would have become part of the family and that was an important issue that we needed to be clear about. And we have an agreement that if, despite all our best efforts, the relationship failed that I would still be around for the children. That's sort of an insurance policy in the background, but it's not going to happen.

Pam, 40, now separated from Rhona, 25, and their son, Nicky, 6. Bristol.

Rhona and I didn't plan co-parenting at all. She already had Nicky and he lived with her mother. When we moved in together he would visit at weekends and one day Rhona said, 'Well, he might as well stay.' So he did. We hadn't talked about any arrangements or how we would share the workload, what he would call us, what we would tell the school, and so on. So there was a lot of misunderstanding. It also didn't help that Rhona was unclear about her sexuality. She didn't define herself as a lesbian; she had had a relationship with a man and got Nicky as a result. All of this uncertainty and lack of decision-making has continued and now that we've split up and she's living with another man I really don't know where I stand. If we had discussed what would happen if we ever split up, then at least I would have something definite to go by. As it is I am very concerned about my future as Nicky's other mother.

For some couples, symbols of the commitment to and strength of the relationship are important before considering parenthood. In Sweden, Denmark and the Netherlands official ceremonies are available to register or legally recognize same-sex couples. In Britain, predictably, this is not possible. However, some enlightened sections of the religious community (including the Metropolitan Community Church) and gay secular community (the highly camp, yet somehow spiritual, Sisters of Perpetual Indulgence) do conduct relationship-blessing ceremonies.

Una, 28, partner to Hilary, 34, and daughter of gay father, Jim, 63. Essex.

My partner proposed to me. She said that she wanted to settle down now that she was in her early thirties and she wanted the commitment in life. So, being partly Danish and because I knew that this was legal over there, I thought that it would be nice to have a blessing in Denmark. But I didn't really know where to start so I telephoned a gay help-line and they referred me to a couple of priests who suggested we have a relationship-blessing ceremony in this country. It wouldn't have any legal status (but then nor would the Danish ceremony here), but we felt it was an equally valid personal commitment. We eventually saw a woman priest who invited us to her church. We had to go through various counselling stages and answer rather detailed sets of questions, which we weren't very happy about, because of the sort of questions they asked. They were extremely personal, about everything and anything basically. A lot of the questions we answered 'not applicable' or said that we didn't want to answer them, because they were too personal and she was quite OK about it all. We had two or three of these sessions and then we arranged what we wanted done. I told my dad that we were going to have a blessing and his first reaction was 'Do you know what you are doing?' And then he was OK about it all. I asked if it was OK to have it in his house and he said that we were very welcome. When the day came we were both very nervous, but it was a brilliant day and dad was very emotional about it all. He actually said to my partner, 'I haven't lost a daughter, I've gained a daughter,' and he gave her a big hug, which was lovely. I invited several of my school friends and a very close childhood friend. My partner invited several work friends and there were also 'our' friends, whom we had met during our time together. So it was quite a big event. My aunt had actually met my partner, but I didn't really want to invite her because I didn't know how she would react. My other relatives are mainly in Denmark, but I didn't invite them. They're really countrified people. Their way of life is totally different to the town people in Denmark who are more broadminded. So I thought I would leave it that we were two girls living together in a relationship, and that's all I would tell them.

The ceremony just showed that we are committed to each other. There was a bit of religion in the ceremony, but I'm more religious than my partner, so we said that we didn't want it too religious. I've basically become less and less religious since losing my mother. The church were OK about it because we were honest, right from the beginning.

We wanted to show people that we were committed to each other. We hadn't mentioned children to anybody really. That was just something we've discussed between the two of us. It was important for us to cement our relationship before becoming parents.

Some routes to lesbian and gay parenting are so complex or unusual that negotiating parenthood has many more risks and variables than for heterosexuals. For a gay male couple, finding their intended straight female surrogate mother, setting the parameters and reaching agreements is probably about as complex as it gets.

Jim, 38, single father to Hayley, 8, born to a surrogate mother. *Isle of Wight*.

We decided on surrogacy from somebody we didn't know, rather than finding a friend or relative to be our surrogate, because we both came from families where we felt that it would be frowned upon. It would not be received well at all. So we decided to keep it to ourselves, to keep it as secret as possible. Most of the time we didn't think that it would be possible, that we would ever achieve it. Eventually the right person did turn up, but it certainly wasn't simple.

I raised the subject of having kids initially and Jack took a little convincing. Not a great deal. Perhaps because he knew what impact a child would have. His qualms weren't to do with the fact that it would be two men doing it, it was more the fact that we were living in what some would call a very posh house – very expensive furniture and everything was in its place. I knew what it was like from having nieces and nephews down. . . but of course they go away at the end of the day and everything can be put back. But Jack knew that when you have a child there all the time things are never straight. So his first reservations were of a more practical nature. The lifestyle that we were leading also concerned him. We were going out almost every night and coming home any time we liked. A typical gay relationship. The financial aspect was another reservation he had. Children are very expensive, which I didn't know, I had no idea. I think he also wanted to make sure it wasn't a whim. But I went on for several months, constantly talking about it. It cropped up in almost every conversation we had. So, after a few months it was apparent that I wasn't going to change my mind, it was something I really wanted, and he said 'OK lets go for it.' Finding a surrogate mother was the only way we could think of having a baby. We didn't want to co-parent with a woman after the birth – Jack and I wanted a child of ours to bring up together. There was no way we could approach anyone we knew to be a surrogate mother. We did think about adoption and we even made some enquiries through the social services, as a same-sex couple. We were initially going to go down those lines until we saw a documentary on T.V. in which Theresa Gorman[4] made a statement that no gay couple would ever adopt a child as long as she drew breath. If this was her attitude, it was probably the attitude of a lot of other people. So we gave up adoption as a bad idea, and decided to keep it a secret and become parents through surrogacy. It was being talked about a lot in the media and being discussed in Europe at the time. So we thought that we'd go for it. We didn't consider any legal aspects. We only considered it from the aspect of family and friends. What people, what neighbours would say. It was best kept very, very quiet we decided. We thought it was morally OK. We talked about that aspect. We didn't consider the law or know whether it was legal or not. All we knew was that we wanted a child and that society would not like us having a child. Implicitly we knew that it wasn't illegal, but we supposed that it would have been frowned upon and could get us into trouble.[5] So we went for it.

We started putting adverts in papers, but not in the area where we lived. We went out of our way to visit areas outside London, in the home counties, so we could bring the newspapers back and send off little adverts. We weren't too direct in our wording. I suppose in that aspect we did consider it might be illegal. Also you had to worry whether the paper would accept the advert. We wrote such things as 'childless couple seeks possible surrogate.' We didn't put down that we were a gay couple, but we used the word 'surrogacy' in some of the adverts, though not all of them.

We always arranged to meet people in London and we would go and meet them in cafés or railway stations. We didn't mention that there would be a financial incentive at these meetings, that we were willing to pay for it, but we did at the later interviews. And we didn't put it in the ads. We wanted someone to do it purely because they could, or to help someone, not because they were going to get any reward out of it. We would meet people and go for a coffee and talk to them, and see what they were like. For one or two of them there was no way on God's earth that we would have got involved with them in any shape or form, because of their attitude, their outlook on life, their reliability. They would say one thing one minute and then they would be contradicting what they had said earlier and it was obvious that they were lying. During the twelve-month period we saw about ten people. From one or two adverts we got about four replies, and then in another one, we didn't get any responses at all. We came to the conclusion that the area we went to did matter, people's outlook on life can be tied down to the area they live in, we realized. The more conservative areas produced less response. The more built-up the area, the more socially aware the people were. I wouldn't say trendier. There was one woman I remember and she had four children and they couldn't afford to have another child but she wanted to go through the experience of having another baby. We said no to her because we weren't confident that at the end of the day she would want to give the child up. We also had some young girls coming forward and asking how much it was worth and that sort of thing. There were some that answered the ads that just wanted sex. These women were all concerned about whether we really knew that we were gay, and asked if we had ever been with a woman, and said we ought to give it a try. Had we ever had threesomes and all this kind of thing. I think the woman we chose was the best that we interviewed. She didn't fit any of these categories. It was her first child and we did end up paying her, but she didn't ask for any money. That was decided afterwards and she was quite happy to do it just for the experience. She was a really nice person. She had no hang-ups, she wasn't screwed up about life or morality, or what society thought, or what was right or wrong. She had her own belief system and she stuck to her guns. She didn't have a career at the time. She had been at college, and was working towards an HND or something, but she was prepared to take time out and go for this.

We didn't talk to her about money at all initially, and it was only after Hayley was born that the subject of money came up. We brought it up because we weren't prepared to pay someone not knowing if that person would then take the child away, and it would have been a waste of time. We couldn't afford it, we weren't that well-off. Initially the agreement was that she would do it because she could, and she was more than willing to help. We agreed that she would live with us for twelve months after the child was born. We didn't specifically say twelve months, but it was something like, 'Once the child is born, you'll have to stay with us for a while to make sure everything is all right, and to satisfy social workers and health visitors and that kind of thing.' So we didn't know how long she'd need to be involved for before we went ahead and started trying for conception.

Notes

1. See the 'Summary of criteria, for acceptance as a sperm donor' (Appendix 1).
2. See Chapter 9 for a fuller discussion of the legal implications of same-sex couples as parents.
3. M.B. King and P. Pattison (1991) Homosexuality and parenthood (decisions in the courts). *British Medical Journal*, 303: 295–7.
4. Theresa Gorman, Conservative MP for Billericay, Essex.
5. The Surrogacy Act 1985 made it illegal for money to change hands over a surrogacy deal but allowed non-commercial surrogacy to be a legal arrangement. There are a few surrogacy agencies in the UK who will put childless couples in contact with willing surrogate mothers. Whether they are happy for same-sex couples to be their clients is pot-luck. Much surrogacy in the UK is through private arrangements, which are much more difficult for the authorities to monitor or detect. Advertising for commercial surrogate mothers (where a fee will be paid) is illegal, but you can advertise for a surrogate mother who will not benefit financially. In practice, many newspapers and magazines will not accept these adverts, even though they are not illegal.

FOUR

Doing the Business

For obvious reasons, lesbian and gay parents who have not had children in a 'heterosexual' relationship or marriage have to be slightly more creative about how to conceive their child and/or about who's actually going to have it. As the last chapter shows, a common choice for lesbian couples is to find a donor father with whom they can negotiate the ground rules for parenting the child. So what are some of the arrangements lesbian and gay parents-to-be devise for actually achieving conception?

Samantha, 39, mother to two adult daughters, 19 and 23, and co-parent, with her lover Stella, 28, to Holly, 2. *Kent.*

We decided we needed a syringe and I didn't think you could just buy them, so I tried to persuade a chemist to sell me one. I told him my daughter, who is a nurse, was about to be twenty-one and that I'd like to put a syringe on top of her birthday cake. He got out a box of syringes and was showing me all the different sizes. I was thinking, 'God, how much does it take?' Well, it's not something you measure is it?! Anyway, I picked one and brought it home and said to Stella, 'Well, we've got part of it now. We're on our way.'

Glenda, 31, who co-parents with Sally, 40, their daughter Nerys, 4. *Southampton.*

I used to call our donor when I knew I was ovulating. I would go alone to a friend's house where he'd be waiting. We had to be sure our friend was trustworthy because she would know who the real father of our child was and we had to be sure she would never tell our daughter or anyone else. It was more important than anything to us that the father was not around, or known, after the birth. So, he would do his part of the job and my friend would bring the sample in a cup to me. By the time I was done with my syringe he'd be already gone and I'd come

36

home and say, 'Yeah, I've done it.' It was all a bit embarrassing, which was why Sally didn't come with me. He was quite tall and it did cross my mind, as I'm small, that I'd have problems during childbirth, but it was OK in the end. He was a genuinely caring person; he didn't have to do it. Because of him we've got a child. It took three months. I fell pregnant on the fourth month but I could have phoned him every day if I'd have wanted to. Within three days of conceiving I was so sick that we *knew* I was pregnant.

Gareth, 37, donor father to three daughters – Sasha, 3, Ella, 2, and Alicia, 1 – by different mothers. *Surrey*.

With each of my three daughters the mother-to-be asked me to undergo an HIV test. I knew this would be asked of me and I didn't mind. In each case I was negative, as I knew I would be. In this day and age I think any gay man who is expecting to father children must expect to take an HIV test. It's an essential precaution for the mothers. With my first daughter, I had already had an HIV test six months before I started making donations and I had the written result to prove I was negative then. One of the mother's friends did come to the clinic with me and was present when the blood was taken from me, with my permission. They were being extremely careful and wanted to know absolutely that I'd had the test and it was my blood being tested. With my second child, the mother-to-be and her partner accompanied me to the clinic but weren't present when the blood was taken. With the mother of my third daughter, as I'd had the last test only a month before and I had written evidence of three tests, she was prepared to proceed on that basis.

In each case the mothers or their partners came to my flat to collect the sperm donation. The very first time I made a donation the lesbian couple involved sent a friend of theirs to collect it. Perhaps I was mistaken, but from the look of her, and the badges and so on, I thought she was a separatist or something. The couple had obviously told her to bring a receptacle and she turned up with this litre-size pickle jar, which I used, but it was a bit like Hancock's blood donor in reverse.[1] I came down the stairs and gave her the jar with just a smear of semen down one side. She just looked at it and I could tell she was thinking, 'I came here expecting a pint or something!' and I was saying to her, 'Well that's as much as it is. In fact that's quite a lot there.' But after that incident we used a small pill bottle with a wide neck and I got very skilled at getting it all in first time.

Marie, 34, partner to Sarah, 36, co-parent to Alastair, 12. *Tyneside*.

We had a nice little plastic vitamin jar for Gary to deposit his donation into. We had been told we had to use glass or plastic to carry the semen; sperm don't like metal apparently. Sarah had gone to the chemist to get some syringes and they had been very suspicious, so she lost courage and came home without one. For a while we tried spooning in the semen with me upended on the settee and Sarah 'spoon-feeding' me as it were. That didn't seem to work, so we had to think again. Sarah would go and collect the sample after work and get on the train with the vitamin jar stuck under her arm to keep it warm and hoping it wouldn't break. Once she brought a sample back tucked in her bra and it popped out in the middle of the train carriage. God knows what people thought. We shouldn't have used a clear jar, I suppose. I know it's a cliché, but we finally gave it a go. I had a turkey baster which *had* been used for its intended purpose, so I tried to sterilize it and it melted and went a very strange shape. . . but it worked. . . first time! That's how I finally became pregnant.

Derek, 42, donor father. *London*.

I don't know if I can really be called a donor father. I also have a problem with why we conceived the child the way we did. A female friend of mine, whom I'd known since I was at school, said she was now a lesbian and was desperate to have a child. She had been in two violent relationships with men. She wanted me to be the father of her child and wasn't keen on artificial insemination, nor did she know how to go about it anyway. I tried to talk to her about how some lesbian friends of mine had achieved pregnancy, but she was adamant that she wanted a natural conception. So, reluctantly, and after many months of persuasion, we started trying to conceive a baby the conventional way. On both sides, I think we may have done it because we were still working through some doubts and unhappiness with our own sexualities. Now I define myself as gay, but back then, in the late 1970s, I didn't really refer to myself as anything. I knew I was only attracted to men, but calling yourself gay wasn't common then. On her side, I think she hoped we might both be converted to heterosexuality. I think she was hoping that a sensitive, softly-spoken man like me whom she'd known so well, for so long, could be an acceptable partner and would allow us both to be ourselves as well as appear conventional. My friends say she was in love with me. I also think she lied about when she was in her fertile times because it took months and months for her to conceive. I can't believe how gullible I was. I also don't know how I managed to have sex with her so often. I didn't find it erotic or exciting at all. Sometimes it took a lot of 'persuasion' to achieve orgasm, but I sort of got used to it and viewed it like an experiment almost. When she finally became pregnant, I breathed a huge sigh of relief. I haven't had sex with a woman since; that's over fifteen years ago now.

Simon, 38, and his lover Giles, 43, with Nita, 37, and Cheryl, 39, are co-parents to James, 8, and Edward, 6. *Kent*.

I was the donor for our first son, but there's no paternity on the part of myself or my partner for our second child. The other mother is black, and she wanted a black partner, so we couldn't measure up because we weren't the right colour. So with our second son there is no known father because he was a sperm-bank child, and there is no co-parenting arrangement there with the natural father at all. At the time they didn't seem to have any difficulty getting AID (artificial insemination by donor) from a sperm bank even though they were openly lesbian. But I think things have changed since, I think they would have problems with some clinics now.[2]

Jim, 38, single father to Hayley, 8, born to a surrogate mother. *Isle of Wight*.

Frances, our surrogate mother, moved in with us before we started trying for the baby. It turned out to be a year before Hayley was born because Frances didn't conceive straight away. It took three months for her to become pregnant. We all three went up to London and had a health screening and we were all clear. AIDS was never an issue for Jack and me anyway, because we had been together monogamously since 1980.

Jack and I didn't decide who was going to be the father. We decided we didn't want to know who the father is. It's one of us, but we don't know which one. Semen from both of us was used. We came into the same jar and mixed up our sperm for Frances to use and off she went into her room with the jar and a large syringe. Some people say Hayley looks like Jack, and others think that she looks like me, but I don't want to know now. I couldn't bear the thought of her not being mine if I did have a blood test done, but also, what does it matter? Jack has left now and Hayley is very much my daughter, whoever the natural father actually is.

Belinda, 36, and Jane, 34, mothers to Alice, 2. *London.*

I tried on and off for five years with a progressive fertility clinic and for most of that time I was on my own. It was a useless arrangement. I was sub-fertile and wasn't helped to do something about it quickly enough by the clinic, but they were quite happy to take my money. I realized then that I should try to get a 'live' donor to see if that would work; so I did, but it all felt a bit dodgy. He was in one of the caring professions and I'd done the right thing and found him through *City Limits* and not *Time Out*, but I still felt uneasy about him. I couldn't quite put my finger on why. But that was a good enough reason to stop. Then I started taking all sorts of nasty carcinogenic drugs to improve my fertility. When I met Jane, six years ago, she had no intention of having a baby. It had never been a dream of hers for a relationship. She freaked out and so I dropped the subject. A year into our relationship I brought the subject up again and we went back to the same insemination clinic and after weeks and weeks of donor inseminations and drug treatments they advised us to give it a rest for a while. After a year and a half we decided to try and find another 'live' donor father. We tried to advertise in a popular London magazine, but they wouldn't accept an ad for sperm donors and sent us a solicitor's letter rejecting the ad. It seemed rather incredible given some of the other stuff in the magazine. So we were rather cheeky and wrote to some of the women who had advertised in another paper for sperm donors, asking if they would send us their rejects. That's how we found our donor, Gary. There was nothing undesirable about him; he just lived too far away from the women he'd originally written to. Before Gary, though, we saw a straight man who lived near us, but he seemed a little strange as we got to know him. He was incredibly shy and maybe this was his only way of having some kind of relationship or achieving parenthood. We didn't fancy years of contact on that sort of basis so we then chose Gary. Sometimes we would go over to his place or he would come over to us. It was the first time in my whole five years of trying that it didn't feel sordid. It all seemed so clean and adult. But still I didn't conceive. So I finally had investigative surgery to find out what my fertility problem was and after five years of heartache and failing to get pregnant, my fertility problem was sorted out and I became pregnant at the very next attempt.

Maggie, 36, and Shelley, 40, mothers to twins, 4. *London*.

I very rarely tell people how I got pregnant. Primarily because of benefits. I never anticipated that I would always be in paid employment. And if I were ever to go on benefits, I would need to give the name of the biological father and the biological father would have to give me maintenance money. And if I were to say that it was somebody I didn't know then theoretically they could withhold benefits. And so I almost never tell people how I got pregnant. If I told you that, that would mean that I would be withholding information from the DSS [Department of Social Security]. And if I told you I knew who it was, then they would do me for not telling them. I do think that they go to quite extreme lengths to ask people, their friends and colleagues, about whether the story that they have given is true. And I hope that neither of us end up relying on benefits. But we can't guarantee that we won't. Who can these days? The Child Support Agency would try and pursue the father for maintenance payments if we were on benefit. Now they won't bother trying to do this while I am in employment because it isn't in their interests, they are not trying to chase people who don't want to be chased. But if I was to say that I knew the biological father, and I was on benefits, then they would definitely go after him. And if I was to knowingly withhold the name, if I was to say to you, I do know who the biological father was, they would then feel that they had the right to withhold benefits as a matter of course. And I'm not prepared to do that. The public story that I've always given, as a matter of principle, is that the biological father is not around and I won't tell anybody whether or not I know who it is, whether it is by artificial insemination or whether I had sex with somebody or anything really.

Lorraine, 39, and Rachel, 46, are mothers to Sarah, 13. *Manchester.*

We had heard that with donor father insemination at home, not through a clinic, you are more likely to get a boy.[3] Apparently, the 'male-carrying' sperm are quicker swimmers but shorter-lived than the 'female-carrying' ones, which are slower but live longer. We were told that you can increase the chances of having a girl if you inseminate yourself the day before you ovulate; then the surviving sperm are more likely to be the female chromosome carriers. Also, we heard the boy sperms don't like acid, apparently, so someone suggested a weak solution of lemon juice or vinegar to douche with first; but I thought that would either kill all the sperms stone-dead or sting like hell – so we stuck with the 'day before ovulation' ploy. Who knows if that's what did it – but we got the girl we wanted!

Notes

1. Tony Hancock, British comedian at the height of his popularity in the 1960s. In his celebrated 'Blood Donor' sketch he assumes the initial thumb-prick blood sample taken is the full donation and is aghast when the doctor tells him he intends to take a pint of blood.
2. Under the terms of the Human Fertilization and Embryology Act (HFEA) 1990, donor insemination by recognized Donor Insemination Clinics (sperm banks) is governed by strict rules. There is nothing in the Act to exclude single women or lesbians from using donor insemination clinics but in practice some clinics do refuse to inseminate these women. Many clinics also refused before the new Act, but now they have a responsibility to 'pay attention to the prospective mother's ability to meet the child's needs . . . and, where appropriate, whether there is anyone else . . . willing and able to share the responsibility for meeting those needs.' The Pregnancy Advisory Service in London is one of the clinics that have publicly stated they operate a non-discriminatory service.
3. E. Noble (1987) *Having Your Baby by Donor Insemination.* Boston: Houghton Mifflin, pp.103–15. This book suggests that two-thirds of home donor inseminations lead to boy children and corroborates the folklore that earlier insemination and increased vaginal acidity can favour the conception of a girl.

FIVE

Swelling with Pride

However proud or excited prospective lesbian and gay parents might be once the baby is conceived, the growing evidence over the following nine months can increase that sense of pride or become an ever more difficult secret to keep hidden.

Shona and Theresa, 34, are mothers to Sam, 7. *Tyneside*.

Within three days of conceiving I was so sick that we *knew* I was pregnant. I wanted to tell everyone; I was so happy. I was so proud to be pregnant. I wanted this big lump out in front of me, I couldn't wait to be strutting it around the town, thinking, 'Look at me, I'm a lesbian and I've got a baby inside me. We've done it! So stick that in your pipe and smoke it.' But we decided to keep it quiet for three months. In fact we managed two minutes before we phoned our best friends at 7.50 a.m. that morning.

Glenda, 31, who co-parents with Sally, 40, their daughter Nerys, 4. Southampton.

Soon after becoming pregnant I told my mum. I thought she'd be nasty and abusive, just like when she threw me, Sally and all my things out of her house when I came out to her. So we took Sally's younger daughter (whom she had when she was married). She was seventeen at the time and we thought my mum wouldn't blow up so much in front of someone else; and also it showed that Sally was already a good mother, so what was there for my mum to worry about? I know it can be risky to get too upset so early in a pregnancy so I didn't want a scene. Anyway, my mum was fine about it, cool but fine, and my dad was thrilled to pieces that I was pregnant. He'd known all along that I was gay and he'd never said a word till then. I asked him why the hell he hadn't said something before now. He said, 'Well, you were happy and that's all that counted. What would I have said?' I think his silence for so long is cheap. He's scared of my mum. He's a big man and my excuse for him has been that he's just been trampled on for so many years, but it's not good enough really. I could have had someone to talk to in those lonely isolated times. Anyway, he was really happy about things when I became pregnant, it was my mum who was to be the real problem when the baby came.

Samantha, 39, mother to two adult daughters, 19 and 23, and co-parent, with her lover Stella, 28, to Holly, 2. *Kent.*

A lot of people knew we were together and thought it was great we were having a baby. The people who didn't know we were a couple took it for granted that Stella had slept around or got caught out. They thought I was being very good letting this poor girl stay with me. It's incredible how stupid some people can be. I was working at the time and Stella always picked me up after work, and my boss would say how nice she thought it was to have such a good friend, thinking we were just good mates. We tried to tell her when Stella was pregnant, but we didn't use the word lesbian, and she still didn't catch on. Her brother is gay and he knew about us, but she didn't cotton on. I even said to her that I was too old to have the baby and wanted one, so Stella was having it and we were all going to live together as one happy family. She hasn't twigged to this day. We still see her twice a week and she often says things to Stella that show she still thinks Stella's a glorified lodger at my place. Quite an achievement!

Mary, 27, now the single parent of Paul, 3. *Liverpool.*

My brother told me I was perverted when I told him I was pregnant and that Tracy and I were going to bring up the baby together. Then he walked out in a real temper. What I didn't know was that a friend of ours, who is a counsellor, took him to one side about a week later and asked him if he thought I had the right to tell him who he should sleep with. He said, 'No, of course not.' So she asked him, 'Don't you think it's the same for your attitude to Mary? She's still your sister.' A few weeks later I was walking in the town centre and I saw him coming towards me. I thought, 'Oh no. I'm gonna get my head kicked in.' He came up to me and said, 'All right? Come and have a look at my new car!'

He's been fine ever since.

Siobhan, 41, has two adult daughters from a previous marriage and now, with her partner Linda, co-parents Linda's daughter Arlene, 4. *Colchester.*

My ex-husband found out through my eldest daughter that Linda was pregnant. He would almost interrogate her every time she went back home to him after visiting us. He used to phone me up and make snide comments like, 'When's the brat due?', 'It's going to be born with three sixes on its head', and other unrepeatable rubbish. He definitely disapproves, especially as he still thinks I'm going back to him one day. I don't give a shit what he thinks. He's never seen Arlene, we've made sure of that, and as far as I know he's never even seen a photo. I'd like to keep it that way.

Sally, 26, and her lover Jan, 28, are mothers to Lucy, 2. *Manchester.*

The main thing I was thinking the whole way through pregnancy was, 'It has to be a girl'. I wanted to be close to my child, not like my mother and I were, and I thought I could be much closer to a girl. By the time the baby was due we had only got girls' names, we couldn't think of any boy's names. I didn't know if the baby was a boy or a girl before the birth; I didn't want to know. If it had been a boy it would have been all right. I just really wanted a girl. I think a lot of parents are like that, straight or gay. Sometimes you just really want a son rather than a daughter or vice versa; and I wanted a daughter. Thank God it was.

Gareth, 37, donor father to three daughters – Sasha, 3, Ella, 2, and Alicia, 1 – by different mothers. *Surrey.*

When I told some friends about what I was doing, and I've only told some of my very closest friends, all of them gay men, they were very supportive. One or two of them, who are very politically correct and involved in the gay scene, while not being hostile to me said, 'It's a pity. We've fought to get away from the nuclear family that is so oppressive to us and tried to create an acceptable lifestyle for gay men, and here you are just walking straight back into the nuclear family again. Do you think that's right?' Well, I think it is. It has made me very happy and I don't think I'm betraying gay rights in any way by becoming a father.

Jane, 34, and Belinda, 36, mothers to Alice, 2. *London.*

I was excited when Belinda finally became pregnant, but I'd gone through phases of, 'I don't want this to happen, it's taking so long it's not going to happen', and then it happened. Then I had to tell my mother and I knew that that was going to be an ordeal. It took me four or five months to pluck up the courage. Belinda was worried because she was thirty-five when she became pregnant and had been taking all those fertility drugs and having injections, so we were worried every time she went for a scan or a check-up.

Simon, 38, and his lover Giles, 43, with Nita, 37, and Cheryl, 39, are co-parents to James, 8, and Edward, 6. *Kent.*

Once the child was conceived we carried on much as before. The real support was given by Cheryl's partner, Nita. We live our lives pretty openly. Nobody concealed the fact that we were having a baby. We perceive no need to do that in the circles in which we move anyway. We just told people when it occurred to us, as it became obvious or when the subject arose. The mothers-to-be lived in Hackney[1] then, so that speaks for itself, and there weren't any problems. Where we lived, I suppose there must have been homophobic attitudes. It's a fairly genteel part of London, so people don't express themselves in ways that would be noticeable. The neighbours know perfectly well what our set-up is, and they know that they are sort of our children, and they take things in their stride. There seem to be no problems about that. It was all very polite.

During pregnancy, many same-sex couples do not spell out the details of their situation. Sometimes it is through fear that 'the authorities' (such as the social services) will take a dim view, or that their parenting rights will be challenged. In practice, as long as the donor father or surrogate mother keeps to their agreement of wanting no parenting role, there is little that can be done to challenge the parenting rights or custody of the natural mother or father. The choice or existence of a same-sex partner as co-parent is immaterial as they have no parenting rights anyway and being, in effect, a single mother is not against the law. However, such is the consciousness of heterosexual hostility to lesbians and gays having kids that fears persist about losing the children, where there need be no real concern. Even the simplest examples of conformity being assumed and not challenged perpetuates the myth that 'everyone agrees that heterosexual marriage is really the most desirable way to have children', as the following examples show.

Belinda, 36, and Jane, 34, mothers to Alice, 2. *London.*

I wanted us to go to the prenatal babycraft classes together, but when I suggested it, Jane expected us to be singled out, ostracized or at the very least given a hard time. When we turned up we thought our worst fears were going to be realized. They were all heterosexual couples ranging from sixteen-year-olds to early forties and the woman running the class went round the room asking all the mothers-to-be to introduce themselves and their partners. So the women round the room started saying 'Hello, I'm Lavinia and this is my husband James' and so on, and we're both sitting there thinking, 'Oh my God, what are we going to say?' When it came to my turn I still didn't know what to say, but I had to start speaking, so I blurted out, 'Hello, I'm Belinda and this is my birth partner, Jane, who's come along with me', or something chronic like that. They were all staring at us and the woman in charge was trying to be very right-on, saying, 'Lovely, thank you,' but she did insist on saying 'your husband' all the time as if that was the only possibility for having a child. We didn't say anything, and there were lots of people there who weren't married who also kept quiet. Silly really. It would have been much easier for them to have said something than us, but we all just accepted it and in the process I suppose we silently agreed that having a husband was the best, or only really acceptable, way to have kids. Anyway, our worries about being ostracized were unfounded and, predictably, the numbers dwindled over the weeks, but we hung on to the bitter end.

Jim, 38, single father to Hayley, 8, born to a surrogate mother. *Isle of Wight.*

My partner, Jack and I went right through every stage of the pregnancy with Frances, our surrogate mother. She had been living with us since before she conceived. We went to the ante-natal classes, sometimes just two of us, sometimes all three of us. It used to raise one or two eyebrows. We even went in to see the doctor with her for check-ups and things. There would be a different man with her at different appointments, and I think they thought, 'What the hell is going on?' We just made out that we were very close friends, and that we were helping out in any way we could.

With all the medical stuff and hospital visits it felt like it was never going to happen. The pregnancy seemed to go on and on, it really dragged. I was really naive about this sort of stuff. I had it in my head that once I decided I wanted a child we would just get a baby. We were fortunate because Frances was a very healthy woman and there were no problems. There wasn't a single moment of worry on that score. We were all quite young still. I was thirty, Jack was thirty-one, and Frances was twenty-seven.

The added bonus was that we all three got on like a house on fire. No problem. We liked the same TV programmes, we had the same sense of humour, we had the same sort of outlook on life. It was a very happy year for all three of us. Incredibly lucky . . . I sometimes think that it was fate, that it was meant to happen, that it was destined to happen. In fact, I got hold of this book on astrology, which I've never considered to be of any value, and the night that Hayley was born, the planet that represents my star sign, the planet that represents Jack's and the planet that represents Frances's all came together for one night in Hayley's birth sign. That was some coincidence and it sort of raised my eyebrows. Wow! All our star signs merging the night Hayley was born.

We told no one before Hayley was born. Well, not family-wise. All we had told people was that we had this young girl living with us, who was going to be a single mother, and she was looking after our house. I suppose we had laid the groundwork in a certain sense. We didn't know where it was going to go. We had seen similar cases on the television and knew that the surrogate mother could always up and go, take the child, and it could all have been a waste of time. So there was no point saying anything to anyone, because we didn't know how it was going to turn out. We hadn't actually decided how we would tell people we two men had got this child. It was a case of play it by ear. We didn't know what was going to happen. I mean we didn't even know if the pregnancy would come to full term. And I'm a great believer in not tempting fate.

We weren't bursting to tell people either, because there was always the fear that if I tempted fate something would go wrong. I was so happy I didn't need to tell people. The only people that needed to know were Jack and myself. We didn't even tell our friends.

Maggie, 36, and Shelley, 40, mothers to twins, 4. *London.*

I think I knew that I was going to be an object of interest as soon as I knew that it was twins, as soon as I knew I was pregnant actually, because I knew that people would be interested. But it has startled me that people whom I barely know will ask questions. We sometimes feel that we are a one- or two-person education for everybody. I find I do get angry about that sometimes, not very often, but usually I don't mind. I find myself in all sorts of situations giving people all sorts of information that makes you feel like you have some sort of intrusion into your life.

I was at the time living with another woman and we had gone to some lengths to settle ourselves in a place where we wanted to have children and bring up children. We had the conversation a number of times about which one of us would get pregnant. Suffice to say, that when it came to it, that wasn't the reality. I think the reality was very much clouded by the fact that it turned out to be twins. I'd always known that if there was one child, and push came to shove, I could stick it under my arm, put a bag of clothes on the other arm and go off and visit friends or family or whatever, and I'd probably get some support from somebody, somewhere. But you can't do that with two, because there isn't room to put everything. Almost nobody in their right minds would take on two children apart from Shelley, whom I met when the kids were six months old, which surprised me no end. So when it came to it, when I was pregnant, my then partner at one point told me that a woman she worked with fancied her and they'd talked about fancying each other, and I just decided that I couldn't even think about that prospect sensibly and just wrote it off, because there was no point. No point me even thinking it was a possibility. I just had to get through the ordeal of having two small babies. I knew the birth was going to be a difficult one, because it always is with twins. I also knew that the first six months was going to be sheer hell . . . and it was, it was the most exhausting time of my life and everyone else's life around me too, I think. What I hadn't realized was that my then partner was acting on her feelings for this other woman. In the week of the children's birth, she was off starting a relationship with this other woman, unbeknownst to me.

At work I was the first out lesbian in the whole of the council. There were other lesbians and gay men, but they were relatively discreet.

When I sauntered into my personnel section and happened to mention the fact that I was pregnant, you could have heard a pin drop. It was reported to me that as soon as I walked out of the door, six people picked up the phone and phoned everybody they knew to tell them that 'that queer, that lesbian, that pervert' was having a child. I discovered that I was the source of a lot of friendships breaking up, because some people thought it was perfectly fine for lesbians to have children and other people thought that any children should be taken away from lesbians at birth. Some people stopped talking to each other during that period and have never spoken to each other since. There have been some major dramas around and as a result some people don't speak to me still, because I'm clearly not worth speaking to, I'm clearly not an acceptable person. But because it's a local authority I work for and a right-on place, it's been made clear to everybody that that's what they have to put up with. All the people I've worked for have been at least semi-supportive. I don't think they've been quite as supportive as they could have been, but they certainly haven't got in the way of things, and they certainly haven't made life difficult for me. So it's been fine in that sense, no one's ever done anything overt.

Notes

1. Hackney, an area of east London reputed to have the second largest lesbian population in Europe, outside Amsterdam. It is also renowned for its significant community of lesbian mothers.

Tales from the Delivery Room

Giving birth is a great leveller. No matter what your sexuality, social class, ethnicity or the parenting arrangement for your child, the mechanics are reasonably similar. But that doesn't stop some lesbian and gay parents-about-to-be making their own distinctive mark on proceedings (as the following examples show) or, at the very least, keeping the medical staff intrigued, guessing or completely oblivious to what's really going on.

Billie, 38, who co-parents her son Jamie, 7, with her partner Simone, 36, the donor father Mike, 36, and his partner, Mehmet, 31. *London.*

The whole way through labour I could hear Mike, Mehmet and an ever-changing group of friends almost partying down the corridor from the delivery room. Simone kept rushing out to give a progress report every half hour or so. Sometimes Mike would come in, but he's bit squeamish and was worried he'd faint. Mehmet said all along he would not come in. I thought that was fair enough. I didn't want a stadium-full watching after all. I don't think the nursing staff really knew what to make of it all. They were clear that Simone and I were in effect the 'parenting couple' but they couldn't get their heads round the scale of the extended family that was going to share in Jamie's upbringing. Thankfully it wasn't too long a labour, four hours on the slab, as I like to call it, and there he was. Mike was present at the moment Jamie finally popped out. Simone rushed to the door and shouted down the corridor, 'Mike, just get in here. NOW!' He didn't faint. When he went out to tell the others, all we could hear for ages were party poppers going off, laughing and noise, and there was me in agony, nearly fainting with exhaustion, feeling like everyone was ignoring me. I also couldn't bear the thought of the silence if something went wrong. But as soon as Jamie was put in my arms I was so happy that everyone was there and that he was OK. I knew he was going to have a fab life with all these wonderful people there for him. I still felt I'd done all the work though.

Siobhan, 41, has two adult daughters from a previous marriage and now, with her partner Linda, co-parents Linda's daughter Arlene, 4. *Colchester*.

It was difficult for me at the birth because they all thought I was a friend who'd come along to support this poor girl who was on her own. So no one acknowledged the fact that we were together at the hospital, even though I was there throughout. I even bathed the baby after she was born because the midwife nearly passed out. She was a trainee and they were so busy she was alone. As soon as Arlene was born, the midwife sat in the corner holding her head saying, 'I'll be all right in a minute.' It's lucky I'd had two of my own so I knew more or less what to do.

Julie, 24, mother to Ben, 4, whom she co-parents with part-time father, Joe. *Blackpool*.

I'm glad I had the experience of giving birth, but if I'd known the pain that was coming then, no, I wouldn't have gone for it. The carrying and from the birth onwards was great; everyone should do it. I think a man should be able to have a baby. He should be made to suffer that pain as well. But I wouldn't go back and do it again. Especially not now that Kath and I have split up. I wouldn't want to go through it alone.

Glenda, 31, who co-parents with Sally, 40, their daughter Nerys, 4. *Southampton*.

I had no idea what to expect. I was terrified and there was no way I was going through it on my own. Sally's had two so it was great having her there with me the whole time. It went on for hours and hours. Before the birth I'd said I wouldn't have any drugs, but as soon as we got to the hospital I shouted, 'Epidural!' I wanted the baby, but I didn't want the pain. When they showed me the needle it freaked me out. Sally had had drugs with her first baby and insisted on no drugs with the second, which she'd managed. She said it's so much nicer without drugs if you can take the pain. My twinges started at home on the Saturday night. Sally said it could be ages, even days yet, but I threw a wobbler. 'I'm having it now!' I screamed, so she called a taxi and the driver drove like he had six eggs on the back seat and kept saying 'Are you all right, love?' every few minutes. Sally was right that it could be ages yet because it wasn't until 4 a.m. on Monday morning that they decided to break my waters and that I needed help. They broke my waters, gave me gas and air and pethidine. By 7 a.m. I thought I was dying and all my maternal instincts went out the window. I kept shouting, 'Get it out of me !' I was so exhausted. At 8.56 a.m. she was born. I had to be cut, because I didn't have the power. She was so cute; this slimy wet muddle on the table – it was lovely; amazing.

Sally, 26, with her lover Jan, 28, are mothers to Lucy, 2. *Manchester*.

At the moment of birth there were so many people in the room we couldn't really be that close or intimate. They thought the baby was in distress and I was thinking, 'What about me? I'm pretty distressed!' Jan was calming me and telling me what was happening. No one else was. There was no time to embrace when she was born, and anyway I was so high on the fact that we had a baby and that it was a girl, that it didn't occur to me we didn't have any time to ourselves. I'd really wanted a girl and it was my dream come true.

Gareth, 37, donor father to three daughters – Sasha, 3, Ella, 2, and Alicia, 1 – by different mothers. *Surrey*.

I didn't know when my first daughter was being born and had had virtually no contact with the mother after she became pregnant. My second daughter was already two weeks old when her mother told me she'd been born. They said they wanted to feel settled down and secure enough before telling me. I was a little disappointed by that but I think they were threatened by my involvement initially. In fact, the birth was incredibly swift. It's a myth that all first births are the worst. Her mother barely had time to get home from an Indian restaurant and call the midwife before the baby was there; a labour of about two hours. I didn't expect to be present at the birth of my third daughter, but I did ask to be kept closely informed of what was happening. I was getting hourly bulletins from the mother's partner and it was quite a tense time. She was born in the afternoon and I was able to see her the next morning. So I felt quite privileged to see my daughter while she was still in the hospital. Alicia's mother was determined to have a natural birth but after many hours and numerous attempts at induction the baby had to be delivered by Caesarean.

Simon, 38, and his lover Giles, 43, with Nita, 37, and Cheryl, 39, are co-parents to James, 8, and Edward, 6. *Kent*.

Nita was present at the birth. I arrived very soon afterwards, before the baby was washed, but I wasn't actually there at the moment of birth itself. There was no problem me being there, I was just a long way away at the time. I still felt like the classic heterosexual stereotype of the worried father rushing to the bedside. It was very exciting. In the delivery room there were apparently no problems. The child was born in Hackney, which is a part of London in which this is probably not uncommon. And the hospital staff were perfectly all right. It was clear that it was a lesbian couple, there could have been no doubt. There was so much hugging and kissing and not the sort you would expect between best friends or sisters. No one made any bones about it. Having said that, there were no camp touches or extrovert behaviour that might have caused a flashpoint either. We're not camp people. My partner and I are extremely dull gays. We are very ordinary and orthodox, and camp is a little exotic for us, in our dull pedestrian ways. In fact, the medical staff treated me very much as a conventional father. Little did the doctor know that I was appreciating his 'aesthetic qualities'. I don't know what he would have thought of that.

Belinda, 36, and Jane, 34, mothers to Alice, 2. *London*.

I don't suppose we would have got treated any differently had we been a more conventional couple, but that didn't stop my labour being a real nightmare. The consultant said I had high blood pressure and that I would have to have the baby induced tomorrow. So the baby was induced on Tuesday, without success, and through a series of what I can only call butchers, who replaced the midwife who should have seen me through labour, I ended up having three inductions in total, without success. It wasn't until a sensible consultant saw me that I had a Caesarean and finally gave birth on Friday. I'm sure the hospital knew we were a lesbian couple, we didn't cover it up or anything. Because the labour dragged on for so long, we were finally given our own room, which meant that all our lesbian and gay friends could come and see Alice in privacy.

Maggie, 36, and Shelley, 40, mothers to twins, 4. *London*.

The health services were extraordinary. They were fascinated by it being twins, away and above anything else really, and that was fine, they were really no problem at all. I think the reality of life is that most women who go into hospital to have babies do so with the help of other women friends or mothers or family, and I think that probably men have a harder time in hospitals than other women around. And they didn't make an issue about it and they didn't ignore it, they didn't do anything really. It was just kind of like there were women in the delivery room, and there were women at antenatal with me. It was much more of an issue that it was twins. And all the care, all the conversations were about the fact that there were two babies, and there was much more risk because of that, and I was enormous. I looked like a tank. They weren't bothered about two dykes having a baby, but there were stranger reactions from the midwives who came after the birth, who had this obsession with whether I had bonded with each of the babies equally, and this concept about motherhood and bonding with children. Unsurprisingly, they didn't apply these concerns to my partner in the least and that used to drive her bonkers. But that was the midwives, who are focused around mothers and bonding and mothers and breastfeeding, rather than worrying about how the family fits together and works and whether the children are getting the right mix of emotional and physical care. One of the consultants I saw at some point asked how I got pregnant and asked all the intrusive questions that I never answer.

Jim, 38, single father to Hayley, 8, born to a surrogate mother. *Isle of Wight*.

Frances, our surrogate mother, had the room next to mine and Jack's while she was living with us. One morning, at twenty past twelve she came bursting into our bedroom. Her waters had broken, and she'd had a bit of tummy pain, but she wasn't due for another week. We got a bit panicky then and we weren't far from the hospital. By the time we'd rung for an ambulance, and it had got to us, we could have driven there. So we put her in the car, and the next twenty minutes were like something out of a *Carry On* film; there was a post van driving in the road in front of us, and he wouldn't let us pass. What a swine! As we pulled out, he pulled out, when we went in, he pulled in. I was swearing and swerving from side to side, Frances was groaning in the back and holding on very tightly round Jack's neck. Eventually we did get past and we pulled into the grounds of the hospital. I jumped out and ran into the hospital and forgot to put the handbrake on. So, Jack's in the back of the car with Frances hanging round his neck, and the car is rolling backwards while I'm running towards the entrance of the hospital. Jack had to try and jump up to grab the handbrake and Frances is practically strangling him because she's about to have the baby. He finally managed to pull the handbrake on – while wrestling a pregnant woman – before the car rolled back into the doctors' cars parked behind casualty. I wasn't aware this was all going on and wondered where the car had gone when I came out with a nurse and a wheelchair. I went into the delivery room with Frances, but Jack decided that he wanted to wait outside. He'd already been through this experience twice when he'd been married, but I hadn't. I was too excited to think why he didn't want to be present at the birth of our baby. Now I think about it, maybe it was that he didn't feel comfortable possibly being seen as a gay couple. With only me in there with Frances it would be a more conventional-looking set-up. But I didn't think about it at all at the time. I was so intent on seeing this baby born.

The hospital staff didn't ask any questions. I didn't go in the room at first, because I wasn't sure what my position was, whether I could or couldn't. Then the midwife came out and said, 'Are you Jim? Frances wants you to go in.' I had said to her, 'When you're in there, if you can, ask if I can come in.' So I went in and I grabbed hold of her hand and said, 'Push, push' and she said, 'Bugger off!', she was in so much pain. This shocked me, it was very unlike her. The next thing I knew, Hayley just shot out like a bullet. We arrived in the delivery room at quarter past one, and Hayley was born at twenty past one. I could not believe it. There was no heave, push, she just shot out and slid down this table. It was the fastest delivery they had ever had in the hospital. The midwife picked Hayley up. I was standing next to her, and she wrapped her in this thing, passed her to me, so that I could pass her to Frances, because

I was in the way. So I was the first person to hold her. I didn't want to pass her to Frances, but I did.

The next thing I knew I felt I was going to pass out, and I had to leave the room. I went out, found Jack, and said 'Its a girl'. We were in the waiting room alone, and hugged each other. We both had tears in our eyes. Initially, Jack thought something had gone wrong because I was out so quickly or that I was going to pass out or that I needed a cigarette.

It didn't matter if the baby was a boy or a girl. I think if I was totally honest I would have been apprehensive if it had been a boy because of people's myths and prejudices about gays as child molesters.[1] As soon as Hayley was born I wanted to tell the whole world. I really wanted to scream it. That's when it first hit me, that you can't tell the world. It's not like that when you've got a surrogate mother having your baby and you're not sure if she's going to actually hand it over.

Notes

1. See Chapter 9 for a discussion on the research that shows gay men are no more likely to be child abusers than heterosexual men and that there is a closer link between incest and paedophilia than between homosexuality and paedophilia, which do not seem to be linked.

SEVEN

Isn't She Lovely?

The early days for new lesbian and gay parents can precipitate all the unanswered questions from friends, relatives or neighbours who don't know the full story. It is often the time that real disapproval or genuine acceptance come to the surface. Seeing the child face to face, does rather bring out the best or the worst in people.

Sally, 26, with her lover Jan, 28, are mothers to Lucy, 2. *Manchester.*

The reactions to us being unconventional parents started before we had even left the hospital. We were given 'the contraceptive talk'. The poor nurse knew exactly what the score was with me and Jan and said, 'I'm really sorry but I have to tell you this,' and she proceeded to explain to us both the different means of contraception. . . as if we needed it!

Glenda, 31, who co-parents with Sally, 40, their daughter Nerys, 4. *Southampton.*

My mum was very inconsiderate. She didn't send a card or flowers to the hospital. She didn't visit me in hospital either. Within minutes of having the baby, I asked Sally to phone my mum and dad and that was the last contact we had with them for three weeks, when they came down on holiday. The day before they came down I did get a card from them, just an ordinary card with best wishes, nothing over-excited about getting a granddaughter or anything. My brother had had a baby boy six months earlier, and my mum had been completely absorbed in him, but our baby was different for her. When they arrived, my mum picked up the baby and said, 'Good job it's not a boy. Not exactly handsome is it!' I was really upset and said, 'It's not an it, it's a girl and she's beautiful.' My mum said, 'Well, you can't exactly say that, can you?!' and put her down. I'd had enough and told her, 'If we fall out now you'll never see us again. That's it, you're not gonna be up one day and down the next.' She's been fine since. She now treats Nerys like she's her granddaughter, phoning her up, sending her presents. But there's still a tension there.

Samantha, 39, mother to two adult daughters, 19 and 23, and co-parent, with her lover Stella, 28, to Holly, 2. *Kent*.

It was difficult for me when we came home because some people knew we were a couple, but those who assumed that I'd just let this poor girl stay with me were not expecting the reaction they were going to get, so I had to tone it down. I couldn't appear as excited as I wanted to be, so the first few weeks were a bit nerve-wracking until everyone settled down and left us alone. Our friends, mostly straight, treat us no different to other couples, and often ask us to look after their kids or grandkids too. When we go to heterosexual events, like the teddy bear's picnic we took Holly to the other week, we choose not to show we're a couple; we got shouted at once or twice and it's easier not to be too open. I can't understand those neighbours who don't seem to know we're a couple. They must be blind. We go out together, we come in together. If I talk, it's about Stella and Holly; if Stella talks, it's about me and Holly; if Holly talks, it's about me and Stella. But some of them still ask both of us occasionally if we've found the right man yet. Incredible.

Maggie, 36, and Shelley, 40, mothers to twins, 4. *London*.

Maggie: The first three weeks were just exhaustion. I don't remember anything else. I don't think anybody who has twins could survive it very easily, unless they've got an extensive network of family and friends who do a substantial amount of caring or bottle-feeding, or even just cleaning or cooking your food. There were a number of people who brought in food and I do remember that I ate an enormous amount because I was breast-feeding.

I have to say that, at that time, Shelley and I were steadily and rapidly falling in passionate love with one another, and that helped an awful lot I think, because we clearly wanted to spend a lot of time with each other. So it actually made the workload of having twins quite a lot more bearable, I must say. It's very strange falling in love with someone while a baby is being sick down your back, and other such exciting incidents I could tell you about, because it made it very funny. Whereas I think until then it had really been an ordeal, if not a nightmare. I don't know, a trouble shared is certainly a trouble more than halved, it made life much more pleasant. Even the really awful times were sort of, 'Oh well, we'll look back on this and laugh about it, won't we?' and we do every now and again. Even the time the twins were really poorly and we were up all night for days on end. I think life got a lot easier because we were so happy at that time.

I also found myself in many different situations, with people asking for all sorts of information. It makes you feel like they are intruding into your life. You end up thinking you are representing all lesbian parents. If you say something, you have to put the best gloss on it, because you daren't say, 'We had a fight last night' or 'We haven't had sex for weeks because we're too fucking tired,' although that is the sort of normal thing that heterosexual people would say with a new baby, especially with twins. But if I said that, that would give them a funny image about lesbians as parents. I get scared about doing that. There's very few people I actually give the real truth to at all, because I don't want them to think that lesbians are weird or are incompetent parents. I want them to think that we are normal, kind of affectionate, sometimes irritated, parents – the way everybody else is. If I say anything like, 'I get irritated with the children', I don't want them to think that I abuse my children because I'm a lesbian. I just want them to think I get irritated with the children sometimes, just like everybody else gets irritated with their children. I can't help feeling I'm always being judged as a mother because I'm a lesbian.

Shelley: When I met Maggie I went round to the house and I realized that everything wasn't quite so hunky-dory. I suppose at the time she did look very, very tired. And I've got quite a clear memory of the two babies in bouncy chairs being spoon-fed, one of which I helped with, and I was wondering 'How you do this all day on your own with twins?' Maggie, in effect, was on her own, because although her partner of the time was still living in the house, she was around very little. It seemed like Maggie spent a great deal of time on her own with the babies. To cope on your own with the process of double nappy-changing and double feeding, and then some more nappy-changing, and then soothing because one of them cried and then the other cried and so on, was to me mind-boggling. It was almost exactly what I never wanted to do. I thought 'Oh my goodness, here's a woman who needs some assistance, quick give me a baby.' Maggie took one look at me and thought, 'She's never done this before in her life, she doesn't know one end of a baby from the other,' which was true. But you know, you just sort of roll your sleeves up and help out, don't you?

Siobhan, 41, has two adult daughters from a previous marriage and now, with her partner Linda, co-parents Linda's daughter Arlene, 4. *Colchester*.

We left the hospital on our own like any other couple, even though they didn't know we were a couple. We didn't tell anyone on the ward our business. You can never be sure of people's reactions. I was with Linda on the ward much more than any of the husbands or boyfriends. I only came home to rest and clean up. Within a week of having her, it was like she'd always been around. We had said to ourselves, 'Remember, this baby is coming into our lives, not us into hers.' But it doesn't work that way. She completely runs this house. She's just pulled me and Linda closer together if that was possible. We'd been in from the hospital less than an hour when the neighbours started coming in, oohing and cooing with presents. It went on for about a week. Our best friends were so excited. People were amazing.

Simon, 38, and his lover Giles, 43, with Nita, 37, and Cheryl, 39, are co-parents to James, 8, and Edward, 6. *Kent*.

I had quite a reasonable amount of involvement in the early years. I certainly know how to make bottles and change nappies, and bath babies, prepare food for children who have just been weaned, and so on. As far as sleepless nights are concerned, there's no comparison between what Giles and I did and the huge burden of sleepless nights that the mothers have shouldered. The kids live with their mothers, so we've only had a few to cope with to give the women a break. My partner was much better at getting up and hearing the baby, although I sleep quite lightly, but he was more sensitive to the fact of the child crying. When we let him sleep in our room, for instance, if the child woke up in the middle of the night, and wanted water, or a drink of some sort, Giles would get up first, usually. But on the other hand, he didn't like changing nappies, so it sort of evened itself out. There was never any question that the kids wouldn't live with their mothers, so my partner and I have had the very best of all worlds, really. The joy of having kids, the opportunity to be responsible for them and enjoy them when they were babies, but with the bliss of not having to deal day in day out with the heavy burden of constant babycare. We've got a much better set-up than heterosexual fathers, I'd say, and the boys' mothers have two dads who help out when needed and who assist financially too.

Kirk, 37, whose partner Keith, 43, is the natural father to Kelly, 15, and Stuart, 18. *Leeds.*

When the housing association found us our house we couldn't believe our luck, even though it was in quite a rough neighbourhood. Although our kids were eight and eleven, Keith and I had been their co-parents for less than four weeks. His ex-wife said we had to take them because she couldn't cope any more. We were concerned about how the kids would be received locally. Being a rough area we thought they might be picked on because we were their gay parents and known as a gay couple locally. Keith and I do not hide our relationship from anyone. We're proud of who we are and we were anxious about that perhaps causing problems for the kids. Luckily enough, opposite the house we moved into lived a lesbian couple with five kids. They were both local dykes with a very up-front attitude. If anyone threatened their kids they would be out there in the street with fists flying; so the kids were all quite safe. I suppose you could say the women opposite had cleaned up the neighbourhood as far as the risk of homophobic attacks on the kids was concerned.

Jane, 34, and Belinda, 36, mothers to Alice, 2. *London.*

Belinda's mum was at our house when we came home from hospital. We had all been getting no sleep, what with a three-day labour, Belinda had just had a Caesarean operation and was still feeling drained and unwell and there was a new baby in the house who didn't know the meaning of 'sleeping through the night'. Two or three days after Alice was born, there was a knock at the door and it was two of our lesbian friends from Liverpool who had come down, unannounced, to see the baby and were expecting to be entertained. I don't think they could have missed the sight of my chin hitting the ground when I opened the door. They didn't seem to understand we weren't fit for entertaining. After a few hours of us feigning delight, they announced they had booked themselves into a hotel. We breathed a sigh of relief and off they went, promising to return for lunch the next day. I felt like a heel, because obviously they should have stayed here, but we were just so overwhelmed by everything and feeling tired and unwell. It was awful of us really. In the end it wasn't too bad and they didn't seem to mind, but it showed us that our lives would never be the same again and we were never going to be the carefree people our friends had come to know over the years. We never really regret having a baby; we only think we regret it when we've had no sleep for days on end, and disturbed nights. You think, 'Bloody hell, I can't cope, I can't cope.' Alice is very wakeful, we've tried different strategies and nothing's worked. She's not a sleeper; she's happy going to bed at midnight and waking up at six every day and that's not like us at all.

Bernice, 41, and Julie, 32, mothers to Olive, 11. *Cardiff.*

I was seven months pregnant before we said anything to the neighbours. There's an old couple next door who have a tendency to be racist and sexist and take a dim view of us. We had builders here once who said to us, 'That bloke next door thinks you're a lesbian you know?' A few weeks before Olive was born, when I was first off work, Arnold from next door was joking over the fence, asking if I didn't have anything better to do and that I should get back to work. It was winter and I'd been wearing this huge anorak for weeks every time I left the house and they hadn't cottoned on at all. So I told him I was having a baby. He could not believe it and rushed back into the house to tell his wife, Ivy, who's had a stroke and is wheelchair-bound. I heard her say, 'Don't be ridiculous, Arnold. You've got that wrong.' Anyway, they didn't really have time to get uptight about it because Olive was born not long after. They make a point of calling Julie, 'Auntie Julie'. I think it makes them feel better. After Olive was born, he did ask me once if I let Julie out at night, like she was a dog or something. I don't know what they think she needs 'letting out' for or what they imagine we get up to. But they're fine with Olive.

John, now divorced, father to Gary, 11, and Emma, 10. *Hull.*

When you have two small children fairly close together, you find yourself, literally, running round in circles, for hours upon hours. You'd go to work, you'd come home and start to change and feed them, put the nappies in the washing machine, dry the other ones. You were knackered by the time you got to bed, and you'd get up for work again and it was rather like being on a treadmill. Especially when we had two babies. You can cope with one, reasonably well, but even then your life isn't your own any more. I suppose it's a bit selfish, but you're still a human being, not just a dad, and to that extent when they're very young they just take over your life completely. My favourite phrase when people used to ask 'What's it like being a father?' was 'It's a bag of shit.' Actually, that was used against me later on when my wife tried to deny me access to the kids after we divorced. That's not to say that my children are a bag of shit, because obviously they're not, but the situation itself could be described like that, I suppose.

Some lesbian and gay couples follow a particularly familiar heterosexual model.

Maggie, 36, and Shelley, 40, mothers to twins, 4. *London.*

The week of the children's birth, my partner was off starting a relationship with another woman, unbeknownst to me. And I was sat at home trying to care for these two little ones, and even her friends were helping me care for these two little ones, while she was off working, I thought. Some of that time she clearly wasn't working, she was off having a relationship with this other woman. It took until they were about three months old for me to really discover it, and be able to say 'Excuse me, are you having a relationship with somebody else by any chance?' It all sort of came out then and there was three months of turmoil. It was very unpleasant and I suppose I felt like most women do with husbands who do that to them. I knew enough women who'd been in that situation, I'd been around enough straight friends with children, whose partners had left them, either before, during or after the birth, to know that it was a possibility, even with a lesbian partner. We're all only human after all. Children in reality are very different from children in theory and can precipitate certain types of behaviour or disclosure. I wasn't extraordinarily surprised, I was extremely distressed. Six months after the kids were born along came my 'knightess' in shining armour and the fairy-tale is still running.

Jim, 38, single father to Hayley, 8, born to a surrogate mother. *Isle of Wight.*

After Hayley was born I wanted to tell the whole world. I really wanted to scream it. That's when it first hit me, that you can't tell the world. It's not like that when you've got a surrogate mother having your baby and you're not sure if she's going to actually hand it over. The next day I rang my sister up and said that Frances had had the baby, and she came down to see us. Frances had come home with us by then, and my sister said, 'There's no way you and Jack will be able to cope with a baby in the house.' We thought we'd hidden the set-up so well. My sister and I have talked about it since and she says that she was 90 per cent sure and 10 per cent certain that Frances was having the baby for me and Jack.

When Frances came home to us four days after the birth, she left Hayley alone in her cot while she slept in another room. I sort of had a go at her for leaving Hayley unattended. The most precious thing to me, and she was left unattended. The next day the first midwife turned up and I ended up having a terrible row with her and threw her out of the house. She was quite rude and obnoxious. We thought she would want to be alone with Frances, as we had told them she was basically a single mum, so Jack and I went into the kitchen. The midwife marched in and said, 'Come on you two, don't just stand there, give our young mum a helping hand. You can get those pots washed up for starters.' She was just totally taking over, within five minutes of walking in the door. She hadn't even introduced herself. I just said, 'Who the hell do you think you are talking to?' I didn't like her instantly. She put my back up. I said 'Get your coat and just go.'

'But what about the baby?', she was saying as she went off. The next day, a different midwife turned up and was totally the opposite. She was pleasant, she involved me and Jack and asked us questions, and was totally professional. I don't know what she assumed about the three of us. She didn't ask and we didn't offer up anything. We just got the moment right. Nobody questioned it. I think we were just showing such care and attention and everything.

The next person to show up was a health visitor. Frances and the baby were asleep, and Jack and I were panicking a little bit. We said, 'Oh, do you want to come in? They're asleep, I'm afraid, but would you like to see the baby's room?' We were showing off, like you do, and we went upstairs and showed her this little nursery. It was so beautiful, it really was. I was concerned because we had two dogs, and I was worried that this health worker would come along and say that the dogs would have to go. I was terrified about lots of things, her finding out the real set-up for starters. But she didn't say anything negative. She said the room was beautiful, and because we had all the baby stuff all over the house she asked if we minded that Frances had her baby stuff all over our house. We said that we didn't mind, and she had a cup of coffee, looked in on the baby and Frances, and we sat and talked. It was really getting to me, I had beads of sweat on my brow. I thought, any minute we're going to let something slip and she'll be straight off to the social services. When she got up to go I changed the subject and said, 'But what about the dogs?' She said that there was nothing better, that it was good for a child.

The birth certificate was a right fiasco, a disaster. I didn't go down to register Hayley, Jack and Frances went. The intention was that the father was to be unknown, that Frances had just had a one-night stand. We couldn't make up our minds about the name. We had decided that she was going to be called Hayley, up to the moment that she was born – between the three of us. It was to be Hayley or Harley, depending on whether it was a girl or a boy. We involved Frances in this because at the end of the day it was her child. It wouldn't have been practical to decide on Hayley's name without involving Frances. We would have had to do it in secret and in whispers, and that wouldn't have been right. We wanted it to be out in the open. We would all be sat reading a book or something, and Jack and I would be talking about names, not directly involving her, but she could be involved if she wanted to. She wasn't sort of encroaching on our territory. We didn't agree or plan it all out, it was just the way it worked out. But when Jack and Frances got down to the town hall to register Hayley, they had doubts about the name and whether to put me or Jack down as the father and they were having this conversation in front of everyone apparently. I can't believe how no one smelled a rat. Anyway, the birth certificate didn't have a father's name in the end.

The first argument we had after Hayley was born was about who would bath her. In the end it was all three of us. An arm and a leg each. The first few days, we had this tiny little thing, she was six pounds, and she was everything I had dreamt about. I would sit up waiting for her to wake up crying, so that I could feed her. Frances used an extractor so that I could feed Hayley with breast milk. I didn't give Hayley a chance to wake us up in the middle of the night, I was there before Hayley woke, waiting for her. I was terrified of cot death too. Occasionally I would prod her, if she looked like she had stopped breathing, to check she was still alive. Jack and I took turns to feed Hayley but Frances didn't feed her. She stood back from it. She just provided the breast milk. From the moment she came out of hospital Frances just took a back seat. It was really good. After the first ten days she wasn't allowed to do anything for Hayley. So she would go out shopping or take the dogs for a walk. Then she got a part-time job and had very little involvement with the baby.

I didn't really stop to consider her feelings, or Jack's. All I had in my mind was Hayley, she had to be looked after and taken care of and that was twenty-four hours a day. Jack was working too, but I'd packed in work. I'd resigned from my job and I was looking after the house and Hayley. That was a joint decision, that I would take on the parenting role. We could afford it, so Jack kept on working. He loved work, he thrived on it. To be the breadwinner was everything he'd ever really wanted. They were really happy days then. I remember when Hayley went on to solids, she'd be throwing her food everywhere and I'd be cleaning it up and that was just magic. It really was. That word 'magic' became a secret word between Jack and me. We could just use it anywhere to mean 'I love you' and it was great. While this was going on Frances was just going further and further into the background. She was still living with us and things were really amicable. We were keeping her, we looked after her and I'd put a bit of money away over the years, so finance was never a problem. Frances was claiming child benefit, to avoid questions being asked and so she had some money of her own.

Some people in the lesbian and gay parenting spectrum know how to welcome home a baby in real style.

Jo, 29, and Polly, 31, mothers to Ben, 1, whom they co-parent with donor father, Mike, 35. *London*.

Mike had been present at the birth, but was unusually subdued. He's normally such an extrovert, but I put it down to him being nervous or squeamish. When Polly and I came home, we were surprised when Mike said he couldn't collect us because there was a work commitment he couldn't get out of, so we got a taxi home with the baby. I was a bit annoyed about it, but Polly told me to lighten up. Suspicions of a conspiracy of silence only dawned on me as we turned the corner into our street and I could see lots of light-blue fluttering things in the distance. The tree outside our house had loads of light-blue ribbons and balloons tied to it. As we drew up outside the house we saw lots of cars and nearly a dozen of our friends holding bunches of blue or pink flowers in our front garden. There was a banner hung between the ground-floor and first-floor windows saying, 'Welcome to the world, Ben.' My only thought on the journey home was, 'I want to put my feet up and snooze. Polly can take over.' But when I saw all those smiling faces and Mike standing in the middle of the group with tears in his eyes, I realized what a wonderful thing we'd done. Whenever I feel down or get frustrated with motherhood I just think of that moment (the photos don't do justice to the magical picture I have in my mind). The party itself was a well-thought-out, one-hour-long afternoon tea, including a cake iced with the words 'Forget the pain – let's party!', cucumber sandwiches and crackly 78-rpm records on a wind-up gramophone. After an hour, the obviously well-briefed guests all trooped out and left me, Polly and Mike together to get to know Ben a little better on our own. The neighbours still talk about 'the day Ben came home from the hospital' and we can't wait to tell him about it when he gets a bit older.

EIGHT

Give It Time

Once the novelty of parenthood wears off, natural bonds and formal agreements have different strengths and lifetimes, and the degree of acceptance by family, friends, peers, colleagues and neighbours has a huge impact. Acceptance is not a necessity, but it can make a world of difference to how lesbian and gay parents cope in the early years.

Gareth, 37, donor father to three daughters – Sasha, 3, Ella, 2, and Alicia, 1 – by different mothers. *Surrey.*

I have told my sister, but not until all three of my daughters had been born. She was shocked, but said that her reaction wasn't necessarily surprise. Some of my friends were surprised but had to admit they thought I'd make a good dad. I've only told my closest friends, only about ten of them know. In discussion with my sister we decided it was probably best not to tell my mother, since I would have limited access to the children and because she is such a maternal woman we thought it would be more hurtful to her to tell her about it and for her not to have contact, than to keep it secret. I still don't go around telling everyone that I have three daughters as a donor father.

Daniel, 32, separated from his wife Bridget, 31, and two daughters Ruth, 6, and Mary, 4. *Aberdeen.*

When Ruth was three and Mary one year old, my wife and I decided to separate. We just couldn't juggle the contradiction of being in a marriage where we both knew I was gay, where I knew I'd had no love or genuine feelings for her from the start. It was all duty, what was expected of us, what we were called to do by God. But now that we were out of that zealous Christian phase of our lives it was apparent that we couldn't handle the strains of parenthood *and* a marriage as much on the rocks as ours was. I was the only one working and so custody of the children couldn't even be discussed as a real choice. I still feel aggrieved about that. I know in the eyes of the law Bridget would probably have got custody of the kids anyway, but it was a *fait accompli* that I would have to move out, do overtime to pay for two flats and maintenance and not have custody of my kids. Anyway, we agreed a healthy access arrangement and were both adamant that the kids' continuity with us as parents and the quality of parenting would be as undisturbed as possible. I visit every other night, read the kids their bedtime stories and they come to stay with me every other weekend. Ruth still remembers the time when I lived with them and sometimes gets tearful and asks when I am moving back in. Mary was too young to remember anything other than me and Bridget living apart, so it's quite normal for her. Bridget was very frosty, almost hostile at first and would leave the room whenever I came round to see the kids, but now we have a very friendly and civilized relationship where the kids really benefit from both of us.

The worst bit was telling our respective parents that we were separating, because it also meant telling them that I was gay. I went round to my parents, who are very conventional, and told them Bridget and I were separating and spoke loosely about attraction to men, without using the word gay. I was surprised at how well they took it. It helped that Bridget and I had sorted out the arrangements for the kids already so I could answer their questions about that. Bridget went to see my parents a few days later, thinking they now knew the full picture, and was much more candid about my sexuality, and in fact ended up outing me because my conventional parents had not understood from my loose descriptions anything like the fact that I was a gay man in a straight marriage. After that unpleasant experience for Bridget, she said I had to write to her parents explaining in full what was happening, which I did. Both sets of parents were of the same opinion, that we had both been very irresponsible to bring children into such an unstable situation where there was no realistic future for them with both of us. Bridget's father went further and told her that if he'd known the full facts he'd never have given us his blessing or walked her down the aisle. Thankfully, I did get some support from Bridget's brother who was very understanding and supportive and said he hoped I would find a new partner and was concerned about what I was going to do and if I was coping with such upheaval. It's just as well he was understanding . . .

he's a black belt in karate! I still feel for Bridget, we were just naive when we met and she fell in love with me. I feel she's got a bum deal, her world fell apart and she's been left with two children. Neither of us have new partners but she thinks I've got the life of Riley. In reality, all the overtime I have to work to pay for two homes, two cars and two kids while sharing some of the parenting isn't exactly an easy life either. I am still and will always be the dutiful father. She could be a lot worse off.

Gwen, 59, grandmother to Max, 1, and mother to Wendy, 30. *Liverpool.*

Bringing up a daughter with your female lover in Lancashire in the late 1960s and early 1970s isn't an experience everyone could cope with. It was like continual tightrope-walking. We were proud of who we were but attitudes in those days could so easily have got our daughter taken away from us. It was bad enough to be a single parent then, but two dykes parenting a young girl. . . dynamite! We were seen as two friends, almost sisters although we never used to lie and say we were sisters. I think two men living together and bringing up a son would have had the authorities round straight away, but people weren't sure about us, they could imagine we might have any number of reasons for sharing a house and besides all of that, being lesbians wasn't illegal, unlike gay men who were criminals until 1967. So all in all we actually had a quiet, comfortable and civilized time of parenting Wendy; viewed as eccentric but harmless.

Siobhan, 41, has two adult daughters from a previous marriage and now, with her partner Linda, co-parents Linda's daughter Arlene, 4. *Colchester.*

My family totally ignores Arlene. She's not a member of their family as far as they're concerned. My mum's got ten grandchildren and she tells me she would have eleven if it wasn't for Arlene. She doesn't even send her Christmas or birthday cards. No one on my side of the family does. They accept my daughters from my marriage. My mum counts them as her granddaughters. If I had been Arlene's natural mother instead of Linda, it might have been different, I don't know. To make it up to Arlene, we've made sure some of our good friends are called aunty and uncle and come and see her regularly. Also, one of my older friends, an ex-colleague of mine who has her own grandchildren, has become Arlene's nan. She treats her just like another granddaughter. Everyone knows that Arlene has a Nanny Richards; she's even opened a bank account for her. So, Arlene does have a second grandma now.

Maggie, 36, and Shelley, 40, mothers to twins, 4. *London.*

Maggie: I always say 'we' have twins because I have an aversion to being asked who the biological mother is; all sorts of assumptions follow on from that question. Once people know I am the biological mother they assume I do all the nurturing, caring and parenting and that Shelley doesn't get involved in all that. If I was living with the biological father, people wouldn't assume those things and would ask his opinion about the kids. Shelley is treated as not having a real role in the family by a lot of people. Even her own friends will actually refer to me and say 'And how are the children?' and 'What are they doing?', 'How are they finding it at school?', and all those questions. Almost everybody will ask them of me, rather than of Shelley. I think that it is a really strange thing to have to deal with. The other interesting thing about it is that people think they have the right to ask all sorts of intrusive questions, where you know they wouldn't do that of straight people who have families. They ask all sorts of extraordinary questions that they would never dream of asking a straight couple. Like, how I got pregnant, why I did it, who I did it with, when I did it, and what I was thinking of. Why are these things relevant? I mean everybody else, straight people particularly, get pregnant without it being an issue. If I pretended not to be lesbian, or was not so out at work, they wouldn't dream of asking those questions, it wouldn't occur to them. But people ask everything. All sorts of intimate questions like, 'Who breast-fed them?'; and because we have twins, 'How did you do that? Did one of you breast-feed one and one the other?' You get bizarre notions coming out of people's heads that are very difficult to accept. I wouldn't dream of asking such intimate questions. I think that it's the intrusiveness that I find bizarre. I sort of half expected that that would happen anyway, because you get all that about being a lesbian. You get all sorts of bizarre questions about how you have sex and who you do it with and why and which bits of your anatomy you use and what you use them for. There seem to be many more questions around parenting because it's such a taboo. A lot of people think that families need to have a father, so they wonder how we cope without one; who does the disciplining, who does the smacking? All those tricky things that fathers are supposed to do.

Shelley: It's true, people take Maggie much more seriously than me when they know she's the natural mother. I end up feeling very much that I don't really know what my role is. I question it because I wonder what would have happened with a heterosexual couple in the same circumstances. I think it is probably fairly unusual that I started a full-time permanent relationship with Maggie just after the children were born. Most people think that I'm some sort of stick or appendage to the family. They do remind themselves and their consciences trip them up from time to time, and they'll come back to me and ask me some questions. It always feels to me as though that is just in case they are not being 'PC' enough. The people I'm talking about are right across a broad range of people, including lesbians and straight men and women. So it isn't anything that is peculiar to straight people at all. But I do find it particularly difficult, and sometimes it means that I end up backing out of situations where I'm being asked for an opinion about the children. I wonder whether it's going to get worse as the kids get older, because at the moment the kids are only four, but soon they'll start to ask more searching questions, and I can imagine the kids will end up asking me what I am doing here, and what my part is in all of this. I certainly didn't choose to be somehow dealing with society's difficulties around lesbian relationships and lesbian families in particular, and I really don't want to do it. And yet I'm having to do it, daily, because the issues crop up daily, and I actually get very fed up with it, explaining to people that I'm not interested in telling them who the biological mother is, and I don't want to be asked any more. So what if they've got blue eyes and I've got brown eyes? Lots of families look like that too. Go away, I'm fed up with it. I don't think there is anything that I can really do about it, it's just going to go on and on and on. If I'm honest, it's just something that we have to learn to live with. Maggie has to learn to live with me moaning about it and I have to learn to live with people asking strange questions that I get fed up with.

Belinda, 36, and Jane, 34, mothers to Alice, 2. *London.*

We're both working now and so we have a nanny, Mary, who arrives at 8 a.m. I get home at about 5 p.m. and then Mary's free to go. One of our friends had a baby shortly after we did so we share Mary, who brings Sally, my friend's daughter, with her each day. Mary was going through a divorce when we interviewed her and she was very pleased to find a situation where there was no man in the house. We didn't spell out that Jane and I are partners, but we said we both live here and look after Alice and she's fine about it. In a way it's been better for Alice to have a nanny, because if Jane or I were at home we would have household things to do, whereas Mary can give Alice her undivided attention and isn't expected to do any 'housework' as such. It may seem odd to some people that two women both go out to work and let another woman look after their child, but why does a woman have to stay at home with their child? Also, we pay Mary a very good living wage, more than we know other people are paying nannies. Not that we have any option if we want to carry on with our careers. Having Alice has brought us closer together and made us a new unit. In addition to Alice not sleeping very much at all, she also wouldn't sleep in the cot, so we dismantled it and took turns to sleep with her on the mattress, which allowed at least one of us to get some sleep. When Alice was a bit older, Jane and I did start spending part of the night together, but sooner or later one of us has to go off and see to Alice. That could have been disastrous in other sorts of relationship, but it was fine with us. Sharing it so equally has really made us see how we support each other. I have male colleagues who admit to doing very little, or at least a lot less than their female partners. We have a great set-up in comparison, I think.

Simon, 38, and his lover Giles, 43, with Nita, 37, and Cheryl, 39, are co-parents to James, 8, and Edward, 6. *Kent.*

The nature of our relationship was such that we were very casual about arrangements before the kids were born. But in fact, since they've come along, things have evolved really, rather than being formally planned in advance. My partner and I do make a contribution to the children's maintenance, but not as much as we perhaps ought to. The two women are actually quite well-heeled, they are not in a great need of money, but we do make regular contributions. They are also very happy for us to have access whenever we like, so it has all worked out extremely well. The relationship between us and the two women was strong to start with, but it's cemented by having a child, and of course there's been another child since, although I'm not the father. Nita is black, and she wanted a black partner which is something we couldn't quite manage, being the wrong colour! When the women moved from Hackney, where no one batted an eyelid about two lesbians with two kids, they moved into 'very small-town home counties'. They knew the area already because they had had a second home there for some years. Even though they couldn't have moved to a more different place, and couldn't have been a more-out-of-the-ordinary couple for the town (two lesbians – one black, one white – with two sons – one black, one white), their reception from people didn't change a great deal. They do have contact with the neighbours, and it is amicable. They have other professionals living alongside them and they haven't had any adverse reactions. If you're apparently professional, middle-class people living respectable, quiet lives, then you fit in, even though there may be massive differences on one or two levels. There was an adverse reaction on one occasion, when a childminder was interviewed and then, on reflection, pulled out having been offered the job, on what was patently a very flimsy excuse. There was nothing said that might have led one to think that it was because it was a lesbian couple; it may have been on grounds of race, as one of the mothers is black. Who knows what motivates people? But the excuse was flimsy enough for them to think that there must have been something else that was the real reason for rejecting the job. But there have been many childminders since and contact with many neighbours, and there has been nothing adverse or unpleasant. So much for the fears of small-town hostility. . . although I'm sure it can happen. Of the two mothers, it is Nita who has lost her parents. So there is a curious situation where our younger son, a black child with three white parents and one black, has very few relatives indeed. He is a sperm-bank baby, so doesn't know his natural father. His mother has a brother and sister, but they aren't in any great contact with one another. So my second son, to whom I am not the natural father, is a black child with very few black role models, particularly in the area in which he is living. But his family is an extended family, which consists of my parents and nieces and nephews who all consider him to be their grandson and cousin respectively; so he is in a large, loving and accepting family, and he is thriving.

Bernice, 41, and Julie, 32, mothers to Olive, 11. *Cardiff.*

We haven't made plans to make sure Olive has male role models. George, her natural father, sees her every few weeks. We don't have a lot of male friends, but those we do have are 'very nice boys', like Keith and Robert. I don't see it as a problem not having lots of men around. But she's also not worried by men, she relates to them fine. I wouldn't mind having a second child, but I'd only do it if George agreed to be the father again. That way both of my kids would be full siblings, not half-brothers or sisters and they could be real 'partners in crime' together, sharing the same parents.

We did think about moving out of Cardiff, but we have a good support network of friends here and people are more broadminded in big cities, we think. We wouldn't want to be in a hostile situation. I am the guardian mentioned in Bernice's will, but we're not sure what legal standing that has.[1] We have both nominated each other as the beneficiaries of our pensions at work as partners. We're lucky that the schemes we are in allow us to nominate our partners, but it is still at the discretion of the trustees, although in practice they will follow your wishes, as long as they can see there was a dependent relationship between you.

Jim, 38, single father to Hayley, 8, born to a surrogate mother. *Isle of Wight.*

When Hayley was about six months, Frances, our surrogate mother who'd been living with us for eighteen months by this time, just decided that she'd done her part and that she wanted to move on. It was only then we told her that we would help her financially. Hayley was about nine months old when Frances left. We had really grown to love Frances, she was a wonderful person. She had her feet on the ground, no illusions, just a really nice down-to-earth person. We gave her thirty thousand pounds[2] and we took her where she wanted to go. We said to her if she ever wanted to come back and see Hayley, to just let us know; but she never came back or telephoned. A year later we decided to move to the island, where Hayley and I still are.

Deciding what your children should call you in an unconventional family takes some thought too. Unconventional titles can lead to embarrassment for the children in public, but too many mummies or daddies can also advertise the family set-up when one would perhaps not want to.

Samantha, 39, mother to two adult daughters, 19 and 23, and co-parent, with her lover Stella, 28, to Holly, 2. *Kent.*

I deliberately chose for Holly not to call me mummy. She hasn't got two mummies, she's got two parents, a mummy and a Samantha. I'm not her mother so why should she call me that? I'm her parent, helping to bring her up.

Terry, 36, teacher and donor father. *London.*

A complication early on was with names. My son's mother and I agreed he would call me daddy, but with my daughter, her mother uses my first name to refer to me. We forgot to discuss what I would be called when we were talking about having a child. I want my kids to call me 'dad', but it's going to take some delicate negotiation with my co-parents now. It's not her natural mother who is against the idea, it is her partner, who feels, if I am called dad, that it belittles her role as the other main parent. But she lives in the same house as my daughter and is an ever-present co-parent; I don't see how the name my daughter uses for me changes her role as co-parent.

Simon, 38, and his lover Giles, 43, with Nita, 37, and Cheryl, 39, are co-parents to James, 8, and Edward, 6. *Kent.*

There's no paternity on the part of myself and my partner for our second son. The child really knows Giles and me as paternal figures, and calls me daddy in fact, which sometimes confuses people if Cheryl and I are out with the kids: two white people being called mummy and daddy by a black child. The boys made the decision about what to call us. They both call me daddy and each child calls their own mother mummy, and then they call the other adults by their first names. The two boys call either woman mummy quite happily too.

Kirk, 37, whose partner Keith, 43, is the natural father to Kelly, 15, and Stuart, 18. *Leeds.*

Over the time we've co-parented the kids we've lost a lot of gay friends. Not because they're child-haters, but because of the massive demands on our time and the fact that we had less money when the kids were younger and only one of us was working. Also, you get very different priorities when you're responsible for two vulnerable human beings. It really changes your outlook and your priorities. Going out clubbing until 3 a.m. is strangely not on the agenda anymore.

Keith's parents have been fine about it all and are happier for the kids to be with us than with Keith's ex-wife. They know the kids are getting a quality, loving upbringing. My family are a different case entirely. My mother had difficulties with my sexuality for many years but later on was very protective of me. My sister is married to a very homophobic policeman and I know that if I came out to them they would not speak to me and my mother would side with me and lose contact with her daughter and grandchildren. I didn't want that so I haven't come out to my sister and we have little contact. My mother wanted to meet Keith and the kids and I was surprised when her enthusiasm seemed to disappear as we were preparing to go and stay with her. She was unhappy about the kids staying in her house. Keith and I couldn't understand why she was blocking the visit after suggesting it in the first place. Sadly, the real reason became apparent before too long. It wasn't homophobia or getting cold feet, she was developing senile dementia and so has never really known our kids or Keith at all. It's very sad indeed for all of us.

Jane, 34, and Belinda, 36, mothers to Alice, 2. *London.*

She calls Belinda 'mummy' and she calls me 'jummy'; we didn't want her to have two mummies. Having said that, I do consider myself to be her mother too. It's not like I think I've given birth to her, and I've never felt a particularly maternal person, but I do feel like her parent, that I have a responsibility to make sure she's safe and we're doing right by her. Other people treat me as if I'm her parent too, including Belinda's family and at work my colleagues treated me as an impending parent even though I wasn't actually pregnant. I also changed jobs so I could work more social hours as a parent. Some people at work know the full situation at home, others think I gave birth and am a more conventional mother; but whatever they know, they treat me as a working mum, which is OK by me. I was allowed to take annual and unpaid leave before and after the birth.

To have a nanny or not to have a nanny. Not the first question facing most lesbian and gay parents. However . . .

Maggie, 36, and Shelley, 40, mothers to twins, 4. *London.*

I don't know any other lesbian mothers who have a nanny. That was a decision around twins again, because the childminder for twins or two children at the same age is actually as expensive as having someone come in and look after the children. And tons less convenient. We could at the time afford it, we probably can't soon, because they will be at school full-time, so for a long time we just had a nanny who came in each day. That worked very well from our point of view and from the children's point of view.

If lesbians are a relatively small percentage of the population, then lesbians who have children are an even smaller percentage and lesbians who have children who have nannies are an even smaller group. I think what a nanny is, is someone who looks after the children. They happen to do it in our house rather than in another house. That's the only distinction between a childminder and a nanny. I think what's unusual is that we are two working women who have a decent enough income to be able to do that. I suspect that you'd be relatively hard-pushed to find lesbians in a relationship with children, who were both working, who would need a nanny.

I'm sure that there would be lots of other lesbians who would think that what we're doing is not what they would do, because if they chose against all the odds to have children, then what they would want to do is stay with them. I think that that's fine if that's their choice. But we both work quite long hours so a nanny was the answer.

It wasn't actually hard finding a nanny who would work with a lesbian couple. Well, we didn't do the finding, we went through agencies. We made sure that the agency was clear what they were sending their prospective nannies to, and my guess is that they put some effort into telling the women what to expect. I think if you talk to our nanny, every now and again you'll discover that she's had a few problems around it, in that some of her friends, and her friends' friends make comments about it. But she's not stupid and is perfectly able to say ,'Don't be ridiculous, what's wrong with sleeping in the same house with lesbians, what do you think that they're going to do?' So my guess is that there's an issue around some people's perception of us. But she seems well able to cope with it.

Relationships ending are not just the domain of heterosexual couples. Gay and lesbian couples with children also split up. There are no figures available for the frequency of relationship breakdown comparing straight and lesbian/gay parenting couples, though one might expect lesbian/gay couples with children to have more enduring relationships owing to the greater likelihood of advance planning and the consciousness of the decision to become parents. Parenthood doesn't happen as an unwelcome accident for lesbian or gay parents, after all. But long-term research on this question is yet to be done. The uncertainties and strains on the co-parent who is not the natural mother or father can become intense if the relationship ends and access to the kids has not been agreed in advance. It is sensible to discuss all eventualities, so that, if the worst happens, at least there is a framework of stability and both sides know where they are.

Pam, 40, now separated from Rhona, 25, and their son, Nicky, 6. Bristol.

My family were all very supportive of me as a co-parent when Rhona and I were living together. After she was attacked and sexually assaulted in our own home by local lads who had been hassling us for ages, my parents took us in and were brilliant to us. Sadly, Rhona and I split up a few months later and she has since moved about thirty miles away and lives with her new male partner. My parents have been surprised that I've kept up contact so strongly with Nicky since Rhona and I split. They think I'm making it more difficult for myself to come to terms with the relationship ending by prolonging intense contact with Nicky. As far as I'm concerned, he's my son too. I was his mother as well from when he was six months old. The thought of not seeing him any more was very painful. He stays with me sometimes at weekends and during part of the school holidays. He calls me mummy when he's with me and

I say, 'Am I mummy today, then?' and he says, 'Yes, you can be mummy today.' He also asks when he, Rhona and I are going to live together again, as a family. So he doesn't see his new stepfather as a permanent part of their family unit yet. I feel I am really being used as a babysitter at the moment. We didn't agree in advance what would happen if we split up, and Rhona won't agree now to fixed and regular visiting times. I see Nicky quite a lot, but it's when she and her new male partner want to be alone, I suspect. It works fine for the time being, because it's convenient for them, but they could just announce one day that they are moving miles away and there's nothing I can do. Nicky's the nearest thing I've got to my own child, he's really important in my life. He's a priority; in all my decisions he's a main consideration. I know I haven't any rights or security, it'll last only as long as it works for Rhona. I miss him terribly when he goes back after a visit.

Gemma, 32, mother to Neil, 13. *Birmingham.*

After the break-up of my marriage, when Neil was only three, I was so happy when Sue and I got together. We were very good together and she got on brilliantly with Neil. The family home was finally a secure place to bring up a child. You can't imagine how long I'd dreamed of being able to sleep soundly at nights without worrying about when my husband would come home, stagger home was the more usual event, and then often get abusive or violent. I don't know why I put up with it for so long and kept our poor son in that nasty atmosphere for the first few years of his life. Neil hears from his father for birthdays and Christmas, but that's about it. Sue, Neil and I lived together happily for the first few years, until Sue lost her job, and as a result of a long period of unemployment started drinking and becoming less sociable. I wanted to help her get her confidence back , but she wouldn't let me help her. I couldn't believe it the first time she hit me. I thought, 'This is crazy. This isn't supposed to happen with a woman. Especially not Sue.' When it happened again, I realized that I was going down the same road as my marriage. No matter what the problem, you don't attack your partner, and I told Sue that if it ever happened again she was out. At least this time it was my house, I wouldn't have to walk. It took a few months, but it happened again, so I went off to my mum's with Neil and told Sue I expected her to be gone by the time I got back at the weekend. It wasn't quite that easy running off to my mum, because she didn't know that Sue and I were lovers. I had to tell her, I had to talk to someone about it. I thought it was all my fault – why did it keep happening to me? I didn't see my mum that often, and when Sue and I got together there was so much talk of my ex-husband that I daren't mention this. They all assumed she was a mate come to help out with Neil. My mum was upset at first, but, when she saw history repeating itself and me blaming myself for being a punchbag, she just put her arms around me and said, 'There's nothing wrong with you, pet. You're perfect and don't you ever forget that.' We never saw Sue again, and Neil and I are doing great as a one-parent family. He's a really happy kid with loads of friends . . . and he's very good at talking through things. I made sure of that, so he need never use his fists to win an argument.

Notes

1. For a fuller discussion of the legal validity of parenting wishes or judgements for the non-biological co-parent, see Chapter 9.

2. Non-commercial surrogacy, where no money changes hands, which can be through a surrogacy agency, is legal in the UK. Commercial arrangements are, however, illegal. See Chapter 3 for further details.

NINE

Big Brother Is Watching

There are many reasons for the authorities to become involved in families with lesbian or gay parents. Common situations that lead to disputes include: custody battles between a recently 'out' parent and their recently 'ex' husband or wife; hostile custody challenges from either set of grandparents; social services making assessments of the suitability of a same-sex couple as parents, foster parents or adoptive parents; or the same-sex partner of the natural parent trying to become the official guardian of their child. Whatever the source of challenge to the parenting rights of lesbians and gay men, the dispute usually comes down to one of three recurring concerns that heterosexuals have about homosexuals as parents. The popular myths (and they are myths) are that: a) lesbian or gay parents will, at worst, persuade their children to be gay or lesbian, or the children will be confused about their gender and sexual identities*; b) the children will suffer, in particular at school, and in general in wider society, from ridicule, stigma and persecution, because of their parents' sexuality; and c) lesbian and gay parents (especially gay men) are likely to sexually abuse children in their care.

In fact, there is no evidence for any of these widely held beliefs that courts voice so readily.[1] Comprehensive research has shown that, first, children of lesbian mothers are no more likely to be homosexual than children of heterosexual single mothers.[2] Second, they also appear to have no greater or longer-lasting problems with ridicule, bullying and so on, leading to anxiety or depression as young adults, than their counterparts raised in heterosexual single-parent families.[2] Last, there is no evidence to suggest that lesbian and gay parents are more likely to abuse their children. In fact, there appears to be a closer link between paedophilia and incest,

---

* Based on the common assumption of a dominantly heterosexual society that homosexuality is not desirable and that its development in children can, and should, be avoided. The proponents of this myth accept that not all children of gay and lesbian parents will grow up to be homosexual, but they maintain that, at the very least, children of lesbian and gay parents will be confused adults who are unsure of their identity as male or female, unclear of the appropriate behaviour of males and females or unsure of their sexual identity as homo-, hetero- or bisexual. This is seen as either a deliberate act by lesbian and gay parents or an inevitable consequence of homosexual parenting.

and there is no evidence for a connection between paedophilia and homosexuality.[1-6] None of this, however, stops these myths being employed successfully to deny and reduce the parenting rights of lesbians and gay men through the courts and social services of the UK and many other countries. Instances, like the one that follows, from a 1980 court case, still occur, but are less common in the mid-1990s. Gay men still have the greatest difficulty in gaining custody of, or sometimes even access to, their children.

There have been a number of recent successful cases of lesbian mothers winning parenting rights, and with more research now available to back up the credibility of lesbian mothers' claims to be good parents, the trend looks likely to continue. However, the body of research about gay men as parents is not yet as extensive. Many lawyers shy away from advising their lesbian or gay clients to fight for custody of their children, because there is still a preference in most courts for the child to be placed in a heterosexual family, if there is one. Thus many decisions about lesbians and gays as natural parents are still made using an opinion or judgement formed without due consideration of the facts. This can only be challenged by more lesbian and gay parents (and their lawyers) being persuaded to bring their cases to court. With the bodies of research and evidence that are available to dispute the common myths (see Notes at the end of this chapter and the Selected reading appendix), there is an ever-greater chance that the case against lesbian and gay parents will be shown up for what it so often is – simple, old-fashioned prejudice.

Peter, 45, father to Michael, 22. *Midlands.*

My wife and I split up in 1980, when I came out. She got a custody order for our son, with my consent, as long as I had reasonable access. Two years later, after my ex-wife had remarried, she applied for adoption of my son and denied me access, so I refused consent for the adoption. In court, the judge ruled that my consent was not needed and that any contact with me as an openly homosexual father would be damaging to my son. I appealed against this and was granted access, but only if my parents, my son's grandparents, were present to supervise. So I took it to a further appeal and lost. So I had no access to my son until he was sixteen on the grounds that 'possible serious damage', which was unspecified in court – even when challenged – to my son could occur.

Angela, 35, divorced, mother to two sons, 8 and 10. *Yorkshire.*

My husband and I separated very soon after I came out to him in the heat of an argument. He took the kids away, so I fought him for custody. By the time the case came to court I was in a relationship with my new female partner. The thing that swung the case was evidence from a medical expert my ex-husband's lawyer brought in, who said that the children may find my new relationship embarrassing, and it would cause them a lot of anxiety. He won the case and custody of our children. I was awarded access. I still feel so frustrated and angry that such prejudice and nonsense can decide my role as a parent.

The worries over the gender and sexual identity of children brought up by lesbian and gay parents have recently been dismantled by a research study that followed lesbian and heterosexual families over a fourteen-year period.[2] Professors Golombok and Tasker of the City University in London (1995) found that young adults raised by lesbian mothers function just as well in adulthood, in terms of psychological well-being, family identity and relationships, as the children of heterosexual single mothers. Their findings did not support the myth that lesbian mothers will have lesbian daughters or gay sons. They also found benefits to being raised by lesbian mothers; there is usually a more positive relationship between the children and their lesbian mother and a significantly more positive relationship with their mother's partner than in those who had been raised by a heterosexual mother and her new male partner. They also found that young adults raised by lesbian mothers were significantly more positive about their mother's unconventional relationships than those raised by heterosexual single mothers. There is also evidence that their mothers were more likely to ensure they have contact with men[7] and see their fathers more frequently than children raised by divorced heterosexual mothers.[8]

The authorities are more likely to take a hands-off approach where workable arrangements have already been worked out, although the more traditional (i.e. heterosexual) these 'workable arrangements' are, the more they are preferred.

Daniel, 32, separated from his wife Bridget, 31, and two daughters Ruth, 6, and Mary, 4. *Aberdeen.*

After my wife and I separated, we agreed that she would have custody of the children, as I was the only one working. I would see the kids every other night and have them to stay every other weekend. By working overtime I can just about manage to pay for both flats and provide maintenance. Even though these seemed sensible arrangements, given my wife's initial hostility to me after separation and given our uncertainty about the effect on the children, we did seek advice from the Family Liaison Service and from the Arbitration Service. They all said that we'd worked things out very well and that with me sharing care of the children and footing the bills they were quite happy. But I can't help thinking they wouldn't have been quite so happy if I'd had custody.

Another source of potential problems for lesbian and gay parents, particularly those who may need to claim benefits, is the Child Support Agency (CSA). Since the Child Support Act of 1991, all single mothers who wish to claim benefit must name the father of her child(ren) so that the CSA can calculate and chase the maintenance payments he is liable for. It is particularly a problem for lesbian parents, as absent fathers are the main target of the CSA, and many lesbian couples who have had donor fathers (either via a clinic or through their own arrangements) will not want to disclose his identity (or have agreed not to). The CSA will not pursue 'absent fathers' if they were donors from a donor insemination clinic (sperm bank). However, if parents made their own private arrangements with a donor, not through a recognized clinic, the donor father may be pursued for maintenance payments by the CSA. The CSA say they have not yet successfully obtained maintenance payments from these 'unofficial' donor fathers (the implication being they do not believe the father is really a donor father, but that it is an excuse to avoid financial responsibility) but it would be their intention to do so if they could trace them. Gay male couples may need to prove that the absent mother is not a significant wage-earner, but the CSA are likely to be less suspicious about men 'left holding the baby'. Lesbian mothers have also been made to make maintenance payments by the CSA. Some lesbian mothers who either lost a contested custody case or who left the family home have been classified by the CSA as 'absent parents' and have been asked to make payments, sometimes more than they can afford, to the fathers or other partners.[9] If a mother knows who the father is but does not help with the assessments and information-gathering, there may well be a deduction or penalty on the benefits due to her. Unfortunately, personal preference for doing without a father cuts no ice with the CSA. However, proof that the father was violent or a danger is grounds for withholding information.

Mary, 27, now the single parent of Paul, 3, *Liverpool*.

The Child Support Agency called me and said I would have to go for an interview. When I went for my appointment I was led into a room and the door was locked behind me. I said I didn't like the door being locked on me. She said it was to stop other people coming in, but it also stopped me getting up and walking out when she started asking me the most personal questions. It didn't help that she was just like my mum. She started asking me who I'd had sex with, how many times I'd had sex with them, had I used contraceptives. I couldn't tell her my real situation or I wouldn't have got any money, they'd have wanted to trace the donor father, and we'd promised him that he would have no comeback for being the donor. We didn't want him having anything to do with the baby once it was born and nor did he. So I told her I was a non-drinker and I'd had a bit of bad luck, felt sorry for myself and gone out and got drunk. Then I went to a party and, basically, I didn't know who the father was. She asked if I'd gone to the party alone and I said I'd gone with a friend. She said, 'Well, surely your friend must know who it is. Can't you contact her?' I told her that my friend was off with someone else before I got really drunk. The lies I told just so I could get money. I shouldn't have had to tell lies to keep me, Tracy and Paul as a three. The woman interviewing said that if I ever found out who the father is, to let them know and they'd make him financially responsible.

Pam, 40, now separated from Rhona, 25, and their son, Nicky, 6. *Bristol*.

Rhona didn't tell the Child Support Agency who Nicky's father was. She had been living with him when Nicky was born, but he was violent and so she wanted no contact with him. The CSA wouldn't just take her word for it though. We had to prove that he had been violent and was likely to cause undue harm and distress. Luckily the women's refuge that she went to, to escape him, was willing to confirm to the CSA that she had indeed been taken in by them for her own safety. After that they left us alone, and we got the benefit payments Rhona and Nicky were entitled to. One unlikely perk of being a lesbian couple is that if you have to claim benefit, the DSS doesn't recognize a lesbian partnership as a couple. So you both get the single person's allowance, which is more together than the couple's allowance would be.

There are no guarantees that the co-parent will retain custody of the child(ren) should the natural mother or father die. It is not an automatic right. A will explicitly requesting that your partner, whom you also consider to be the child's parent, should be the guardian will help, but courts will always make custody decisions in what they see to be the best interests of the child. The older the children are, the better the case for the continuity of parenting and the strength of the bond that exists between the child and the co-parent. The younger the children are, or the shorter the time that the co-parent has been parenting, the more difficult it is to persuade the courts not to favour the other natural parent or relatives. It is essential to get legal advice in the drawing up of wills, especially when it involves your requests for the continuing parenting of your child.

Glenda, 31, who co-parents with Sally, 40, their daughter Nerys, 4. *Southampton.*

I wanted to make Sally the legal guardian of our daughter in case anything happened to me. We phoned a lesbian helpline and they said that to become a legal guardian involves going to court and we'd need social worker reports and other reports. Well, I don't want them in here nosing around. It's got nothing to do with them. Our daughter is having a quality upbringing, probably better than most. The thing that worries me, though, is that my mother is hostile to the idea of Sally bringing up our daughter if anything happened to me. She said that she would look after her if I did die, and she would take it to court if she had to rather than leave her grandchild with Sally. Well, I'd rather Nerys went into care than be brought up by my mother. She knocked the hell out of me for eighteen years. She smacks my brother's little boy. She told me 'I had to warm his legs up when he didn't listen.' If I caught her laying a finger on Nerys, she'd be flat out. We don't hit our daughter, why should anyone else? So I'm making sure my will makes it as certain as it can that Sally will have no problems bringing up our daughter if the worst happens to me. (See discussion of residency orders at the end of this chapter.)

Kirk, 37, whose partner Keith, 43, is the natural father to Kelly, 15, and Stuart, 18. *Leeds.*

After a few years of the kids coming to stay with me and Keith at weekends and school holidays, Keith's ex-wife came with the kids to stay for Christmas for the first time. We didn't have room for them all to stay, so two lesbian friends of ours put them up, as they have a large house. They visited us in our gay houseshare over the Christmas period and we had a great time. When they went home after the holidays, Keith's ex-wife tried to stop us seeing the kids. I think she was worried after she saw that we could so obviously provide a loving and stable family environment and that we had a wide support network of caring people, while she was unable to keep the kids clean, clothed and fed, let alone the nicer things in life. If we ever had to contest access or custody then we were sure she would try and make a negative issue of our sexuality. However, Keith knew that there was plenty of 'dirt' to be dished about his ex-wife's personal, maternal and professional life, so we got our solicitor to issue a threatening letter about what would need to be aired if we challenged her for access. Unsurprisingly, she let us see the kids again regularly as before and allowed them to come and stay for holidays. The real surprise came two years later when she just handed the kids over with two weeks' notice under threat of putting them into care because she 'couldn't cope' any more. Not the best way to get custody of your kids, but certainly less expensive and harrowing then letting the courts decide.

John, now divorced, father to Gary, 11, and Emma, 10. *Hull.*

When the marriage ended, the kids were five and four. I agreed that the children would be better off with their mother. I do believe that children are better off with the female, call me old-fashioned if you like. But I did want regular access to see the children. It wasn't easy at the beginning, and nothing to do with my sexuality, which she didn't know about. She decided that she didn't want me to see them, or as little as possible. So we had court battles, and I eventually got the access that I wanted, and I see them every weekend now. The courts don't solve anything. Nothing at all. The issue has to be solved by the parents at the end of the day. You can break court orders quite easily; the courts don't do anything. Especially if you are female, they'll leave you and the kids alone very often.

If my ex-wife knew my situation now, that Tom and I are lovers not just flatmates, I feel that she would use it as an excuse to prevent the children from seeing me. Although she's an educated person, my experience after the split-up showed me just how vindictive she could be. Eventually we did reach an agreement. We had to go through the family reconciliation department, or whatever it is called, of the local social services. And eventually we did manage to break through the worst part of our hostility. Now I have the kids overnight and one day at weekends. The rest of the time they're with their mother and stepfather. This is one of the reasons I say nothing and keep quiet, because it makes life easier. She's looking for any excuse to deny me access again and 'living with my boyfriend' would be ammunition to her. I don't want to go back to court to be able to see my kids. She has this attitude that she wants to create, and has created, a traditional family life, and doesn't want anything to disturb that; she wants mum and dad and two kids. And another dad, me, on the sidelines must make life difficult for her, embarrassing. So me having no access would be much easier for her to cope with.

I know a lot of people don't want gays looking after kids because they think we'll abuse them. Well, the view that gay men are the child molesters is in my experience total nonsense. Most gay men that I know want to go to bed with a man. They don't want to go to bed with a child. I think all the evidence, from what I've seen says most abuse goes on within straight families. Anyone who has read anything on the subject would be well aware of that: that the children are molested more by family members or very close family friends, than by gay men wandering the streets trying to pick up children. You get the odd one, obviously, but generally it's a total myth about us.

Maggie, 36, and Shelley, 40, mothers to twins, 4. *London*.

I applied for a home help to our council, which had a very positive statement around equality of its services for all sections of the community, including lesbians and gay men. I got a home help, because I was really struggling at the beginning and not able to cope very well with twins and all the domestic chores. And my partner at the time certainly wasn't helping much, because she was busy doing other things with another woman. Anyway, this home help appeared, and the first time she came she cleaned downstairs and was all hunky-dory. The second time, she put two and two together and made ten. The very next day her supervisor and a social worker appeared at the door. I knew exactly why they were here. This wasn't the normal practice, it wasn't supposed to happen like this, and certainly not in a 'right-on' borough. But I was very pleasant and my charming self and made them cups of tea and waxed lyrical about how I was coping. It was clear they were checking up and they came to see whether, as a lesbian, I was abusing the children. They clearly had their doubts, and certainly the home-help supervisor had raised eyebrows a number of times, and her questions were quite pointed about some things. I subsequently found out that she had been distinctly worried, from her religious point of view, about a lesbian bringing up children. The social worker had come along as requested, and had told the home help and supervisor afterwards that they had been interfering and it was clearly a perfectly fine household for children to be brought up in. I didn't formally complain, but I made sure that they knew that I could have, and that what the home help and her supervisor had done was against council policy. I couldn't have dealt with a formal complaint, in terms of them getting disciplined, at the time. I would have found it too stressful while coping with the twins and a disintegrating relationship at the same time. But I knew it was inappropriate behaviour. I knew it was not dealt with perfectly, but I knew there were words said to them. So it was resolved to my satisfaction.

Some routes to parenthood among lesbian and gay parents are so complex and riddled with potential problems that it is a minefield of guesswork for the parents as to whether they will retain custody of their child if the truth comes out, as this case of surrogacy shows.

Jim, 38, single father to Hayley, 8, born to a surrogate mother. *Isle of Wight.*

Hayley was now eighteen months and here we were, two men with someone else's baby. We hadn't moved to the Isle of Wight yet, we were still in Essex. It was a bit worrying because Frances (the surrogate mother) had now gone. She had written us a letter, as we'd agreed. We had decided to play on the (untrue) fact that she was suffering from postnatal depression, and that she didn't consider Hayley to be her child. Jack and I said we tried everything to encourage Frances to stay with the child, but she had just upped and left. She actually went to a solicitor and got a letter drafted up to say that she was going away for an indefinite period and would leave us as the child's guardians, until she came back; and then she left. A social worker came down to see us once we'd reported the facts. We produced the letter, which she took away. When she came back a week later she said everything was fine, the child could not be better looked after and the social services department had no problems with her staying here. She also noted that Hayley had obviously bonded with Jack and me and the letter was quite legal.

We were asked to take Hayley for a medical check-up and the doctor thought we were brilliant and he was very supportive. I don't know if he thought Jack and I were a couple. I didn't stop to think about it. I'm pretty naive about people. I'm pretty much locked into my own little world, especially where Hayley's concerned.

A few months later we moved here to the Isle of Wight. We had to go through this business with the letter again because of the health visitors. Here we were, two gay men with somebody else's child, and the appointment with the health visitor was really worrying me. First the health visitor sent us a card saying, 'Please contact us', but we didn't; we just ignored it. We didn't want any contact with them, we just wanted to be left alone. Some weeks later a card was dropped through the door while we were out, but again we ignored it. By this time I had to get a job because the money had run out. I was working full-time and Hayley was sent to a childminder. The health visitor was crafty because she turned up at the childminder's. All she said was that Hayley had to go for a check-up. So the childminder took her down to the clinic and that was the end of it. Hayley was given a clean bill of health and they left us alone.

We assumed that there would be all these problems because it was someone else's child, but that was it. They were easily satisfied and we were settled. I had been dreading moving, with all the fears I had about what the authorities would say, and in the end it was so easy. But we did lie when we moved in. We told all the neighbours that we were brothers and that Hayley was our sister's child. They believed it, but they all know the real situation now.

There have been some positive developments for lesbian and gay parents, especially for the same-sex partner who is not the biological mother or father of the children. The Children Act 1989 no longer uses the notion of custody, instead it talks of parental responsibility, and allows courts to grant residence orders (that bestow automatic parental responsibility) and contact orders that enable access to children. It is in the area of residence orders that a number of recent celebrated cases have been won. In October 1995, two lesbian couples, one in Manchester and one in London, were granted residence orders. In practice, for the Manchester couple this means that the non-biological mother in the couple now also has parental responsibility for the upbringing of her partner's child. The London couple, who are each the biological mother of one child, applied for, and were granted, residence orders for each other's children. This now means they are both equally parents of both children, and if one of them dies before the children are both sixteen, then the other will not have to worry about any challenge to her right to parent both children. This is no guarantee of success though. There have been a number of lesbian co-parents whose residence order applications have not been granted. However, there is certainly quite a difference from the first example in this chapter, from the 1980s. These are also clear examples of the importance of bringing cases to court to win the equal parenting rights that heterosexual parents take for granted. After a successful application for a joint residence order by a lesbian couple in Leeds in January 1996, solicitor Evelyn Norman urged more lesbian and gay parents to launch applications for residence orders: 'This sort of action stands a good chance of increasing the recognition and acceptance of such procedures, and of same-sex couples as legitimate parents.'[10]

Notes

1. M. King and P. Pattison (1991) Homosexuality and parenthood. *British Medical Journal*, 303: 295–7.
2. S. Golombok and F. Tasker (1995) Adults raised as children in lesbian families. *American Journal of Orthopsychiatry*, 65(2): 203–15.
3. R. Langevin (1983) *Sexual Strands. Understanding and Treating Sexual Anomalies in Men*. London: Lawrence Erlbaum.
4. J. R. Conte (1991) The nature of sexual offences against children. In C. R. Hollen and K. Howells (eds), *Clinical Approaches to Sex Offenders and Their Victims*. Chichester: John Wiley, pp.11–34.
5. G. Abel, J. Becker, J. Cunningham-Rather, M. Mittleman and J. L. Rouleau (1988) Multiple paraphilic diagnoses among sex offenders. *Bulletin of American Academy of Psychiatry Law*, 16: 153–68.
6. D. Finkelhor and D. Russell (1984) Women as perpetrators: review of the evidence. In D. Finkelhor (ed.), *Child Sexual Abuse: New Theory and Research*. New York: Free Press, pp.171–87.
7. M. Kirkpatrick, C. Smith and R. Roy (1981) Lesbian mothers and their children: a comparative survey. *American Journal of Orthopsychiatry*, 51: 545–51.
8. S. Golombok, A. Spencer and M. Rutter (1983) Children in lesbian and single-parent households: psychosexual and psychiatric appraisal. *Journal of Child Psychology & Psychiatry*, 24: 551–72.
9. J. Radford (1995) Lesbian parenting: past, present and future. *Rights of Women Bulletin*, Winter, pp. 21–5.
10. *The Pink Paper*, January 1996.

TEN

When Do We Tell the Children?

In an ideal world all lesbian and gay families would be happy to be totally open about their situation, and few would deny openness to be the desirable goal. The more areas of life that you censor yourself in, the greater the stress and anxiety of life become. Not only does denial bring a loss of self-respect, but it also teaches our children a sense of shame and secrecy. But good intentions alone do not guarantee a local situation that makes it easy to be open. In practice, there are many gradations of openness within lesbian and gay families, and in the image that lesbian and gay families present to the outside world. In the accounts that follow, the justifications for the levels of openness chosen are many and varied, and show the sometimes harsh reality of being a lesbian or gay parent in modern Britain.

Siobhan, 41, has two adult daughters from a previous marriage and now, with her partner Linda, co-parents Linda's daughter Arlene, 4. Colchester.

If Arlene does want to know who her father is when she's older, then we'll try to trace him. If we can't find him, we can't. We hardly knew him anyway and he never stays in one place for very long. We had no contact with him after Linda conceived. The guy doesn't even know if we had the baby, changed our minds or anything. He didn't want any contact either, so if we did trace him, he'd have to decide if he wanted to meet Arlene anyway. When Arlene was two, she heard her friends saying 'daddy' all the time so she started using the word. We had to explain that she hasn't got a daddy at home. She's got a mummy and a Siobhan; she's special. We told her she has got a daddy somewhere in the world, but he doesn't live with us, and she's quite happy with that. I don't mind being called most things, but daddy is not one of them.

Daniel, 32, separated from his wife Bridget, 31, and two daughters Ruth, 6, and Mary, 4. *Aberdeen*.

The kids are too young to know. If one day they wanted to know about my sexuality, then I'd have to broach it. One thing that worries me is that my ex-wife blames the break up of our marriage purely on my sexuality, but in fact there were so many factors, religious, personal, sexual and practical, that my sexuality is an easy scapegoat for all the difficulties we had. If my daughters were aware of my sexuality I am worried that they too would blame me entirely for the separation, rather than having a richer understanding of their parents' relationship. It also depends what sort of people my daughters turn out to be. I can already see that Ruth is a much more conventional person who may well see things in terms of right and wrong. Mary is a much more lateral thinker and I wouldn't be surprised if she turned out to be more accepting and unconventional.

Gareth, 37, donor father to three daughters – Sasha, 3, Ella, 2, and Alicia, 1 – by different mothers. *Surrey*.

The mothers of my younger two daughters are keen for their daughters to know and have contact with their half-sister. They see it as their duty that their daughters know each other. It's just as well that the mothers all get on, but I'm sure they would continue contact even if they didn't. So the girls have played together a few times, and their mothers do intend to keep in contact, particularly as the girls get older and understand more. I do wonder if my daughters will grow up heterosexual, and in all probability they will. It's fine whatever their sexuality is, but I can't help thinking at the back of my mind that I hope they will be homosexual; they'd have more exciting lives, I think. I just want to be a stable, loving father, that they feel my love for them is unconditional and enduring. Giving that is far more important than hoping they will have a certain career. If I get to the end of my life and have three contented, happy daughters who are secure within themselves, then my hopes for them will have been fulfilled.

Simon, 38, and his lover Giles, 43, with Nita, 37, and Cheryl, 39, are co-parents to James, 8, and Edward, 6. *Kent*.

The children are aware of their parenting situation, in as far as they know that their father and their other sort of *de facto* father (my partner) live together, and that their mothers live together. They have also been taken on Gay Pride,[1] and have had it explained as a festival to celebrate the lives of men who love men and women who love women, who choose to live together. So they know that. My younger son also knows his natural father is not someone we know (he is a sperm-bank child) and he's quite happy with those facts. He's fortunately a very easy-going child. There may be problems in the future, but currently there doesn't seem to be a problem. I think their notions of sex are, as yet, very limited to saying rude words and things like that, so I don't think that they have any real understanding of the implications. I remember once when we were talking about something, I happened to use the word lesbian, and the older boy's ears pricked up. So clearly he knows that it means something of relevance. What it means to him, I don't know. But I believe you have to let them know what's really going on. We're not ashamed, so why should we make them ashamed? If we were to go into the closet it would be pointless, because our living arrangements would betray us, and if they didn't, our friends would provide ample evidence to the contrary. No, the children are going to have to live with the fact that their parents are perverts. We do discuss feelings. The mothers are particularly good, they are both well-educated women and they both have a strong sort of awareness of social sciences, apart from being naturally warm and understanding individuals. I think that this has led to a considerable degree of openness. The children do feel able to express their own feelings, and negotiate their feelings, as it were. Of course they are still very young, and it's very difficult to say, but I do think that they will always be able to address problems or feelings that they might have as a result of being children of this sort of arrangement. An interesting perspective on this is that a lot of children, not only at their school, but children that they know, come from other than conventional homes; broken homes, some have single parents, and mixed-race homes, and so on. So the notion of this ideal, this ordinary family, is a little exotic. Perhaps that mitigates the potential problems that we might have.

Kirk, 37, whose partner Keith, 43, is the natural father to Kelly, 15, and Stuart, 18. *Leeds.*

Keith and I are very proud of who we are and have never made any secret of our relationship and our status as two gay men co-parenting Keith's children. The kids knew all about our relationship for years before they came to live with us. Even so, we talked a lot about it in the first few years, and then it became a low priority and we just get on with our lives. People in the neighbourhood were intrigued by our set-up and we weren't hiding things. They saw we had kids and asked questions, and we would answer them honestly. Both of us and the kids made friends in the area and I used to cook a lot; we had kids round all the time. I'd make curries and biscuits and things, and the kids would go home happy and tell their parents about us. We think it is important to be part of the community we live in. However, we were worried for the kids' safety in the reasonably tough area we live in, where being the kids of queer parents could make them a target. In practice, however, it is Keith and I who have been on the receiving end of confrontations and violence in the neighbourhood. We've had the occasional anti-gay comment in the shops or pubs, but we always challenge it and make it clear that it's their problem, not ours, if they don't like it. Being out and proud, we have been known to walk back from the local pub hand in hand once in a while. It was the opening night of a play I was in at the city's theatre, and we had gone for a drink at our local with some neighbours who'd been to see the play. On our way home at about 1 a.m. we noticed a car was following us. We were holding hands and the two young men driving and the young women in the back seat had obviously spotted this. They eventually drove the car onto the pavement in front of us and the men jumped out and tried to attack us. Keith and I are not small and we managed to frighten them off, but I did get kicked in the throat and spent Sunday in hospital and four days out of the theatre. The police were brilliant and very supportive and took the investigation very seriously. We told the kids about it; it is so important to live with truth and integrity. If we are secretive about ourselves, it will breed a sense of shame for the children, when there's nothing to be ashamed of.

John, now divorced, father to Gary, 11, and Emma, 10. *Hull*.

As far as my children are concerned, I'm not sure what they think. I think they are still young enough to think that we are just friends. Tom and I don't sleep together while they are here. We have our own rooms when they're around, so there are no obvious signs for the children when they come. But as they get older, you can't hide something like that forever. When the kids are about to arrive, I usually go around the house and make sure that all my things are in my bedroom, that there is nothing of mine in my partner's bedroom. Any gay material gets put in a filing cabinet, which is locked. Everything is shoved in there out the way, so that they would never come across anything that would suggest that there's anything other than a straightforward friendship. And generally, we clean the house before they arrive, for some strange reason. It's a habit I suppose, part of the process of 'putting things away'. We make it appear like we're two friends living together. Last summer I remember my son, Gary, wandering into Tom's bedroom and seeing my jeans and underpants on the floor on the far side of the bed. Tom hadn't looked properly when he'd tidied up the room. Gary asked me later, 'Dad, what were your trousers and pants doing in Tom's room?' I said something about changing in Tom's room because the window cleaner was doing the windows in my room at the time. It's all I could think of out of the blue like that. So it's obviously a question in their minds; no doubt planted there by their mother. I'm not worried about them finding out or telling anyone, but I'd prefer to actually tell them myself, I don't want them to find out another way. My wife would probably deny me access if she knew; she's looking for any excuse to stop me coming round or the kids coming here. But it's a question of when to tell the kids, and I have two views on that one. Either you tell them when they are young, and they grow up with it, or you leave it till they get older. Children can be very cruel. I know from experience, at school for example, kids'll say things like, 'Your dad's a queer'. I don't want them to go through that experience. I don't want them to know at the moment, but when they get older, I shall tell them. I'm sure they'll be shocked initially, but hopefully it won't make any difference at the end of the day. If it does it's just bad luck.

I keep telling them how lucky they are, they get twice the value than if they were still in a sort of one-to-one happy family. Sometimes I like being a dad. It's great to see them, but I also say it's great when they go, because then you can have your life back without being sort of shackled. You get used to it – being a part-time dad – it's not easy to start with, but six years down the line, it's just part of life. They come here and they do things and they try things out with me, and I'm quite well aware of what's going on, that they wouldn't dare do it at home. They try things out to see how I react compared to their mum, and you try to be fairly laid back with them, but then you draw the line at certain points and I do smack them occasionally, not very often, but I do now and again, when it's necessary.

Maggie, 36, and Shelley, 40, mothers to twins, 4. *London*.

We were always going to be totally open with our kids, and as we're lesbians we chose to give the children some sort of a peer group. Therefore, we've moved to an area of London where there are other lesbian parents, because we wanted both us and our kids not to be too unusual, and not to face the real hostility that I think we would get outside even this part of London. That's what we would anticipate; having to deal with real aggression, which we haven't had to do round here. That was quite a deliberate choice. We did live in a different bit of London before, where to our knowledge there were no other lesbian mothers with children around the same sort of age, and there certainly wouldn't have been at the local schools. So we've made a choice to live in London, which is not where we come from. We both come from up north, and both of our sets of parents have died. We have a mixed bunch of family, in that some of them are praying for us, and some of them are extraordinarily nice, but live a long way away, and some of them actually come and stay with us occasionally. But we're less in touch with our biological families than your average heterosexual family, and therefore we have had less support from them. So it's become very much us in isolation. We are a bit short of the support network that you often get. I suspect that if my mother had been alive, she would have been supportive, and wanting to look after the kids and help with them. The fact that we're lesbians wouldn't have put her off one little bit. But she would have been a very long way away and therefore very limited, because we wouldn't have chosen to live anywhere but here. It's a real shame that there are some parts of the family that aren't closer. It's a shame for our children, it's also a shame for their children. The fact that the family network isn't there is something we both miss, but there you go, you can't have everything in this life.

Pam, 40, now separated from Rhona, 25, and their son, Nicky, 6. *Bristol.*

Nicky knows that Rhona and I lived with him as two mummies. But now that we've split up, Rhona has a new male partner, so Nicky has a stepfather. We lived on a rough estate when we were together, and we got a lot of name-calling from local gangs. We were very worried about Nicky, once he was old enough to go out on his own, that he would be bullied, especially as he knew the full situation and is very protective of us. A lot of it was because we were a lesbian couple, but it was a dangerous area no matter who you were. Rhona had been mugged more than once. They even stole her mountain bike by knocking her off it while she was cycling. The last straw came when Rhona came home one day to find some lads burgling the house. They could easily have run out the back door when they heard her, they had left it open, but they chose to stay and attacked her, then they sexually assaulted her. It wasn't rape, but it was too much for us to put up with. We packed up and moved within a few days. We couldn't live in a place where none of us were safe, because of who we are. We moved in with my parents in a tiny town in the countryside, where you'd expect hostility and coldness from people, but quite the opposite was the case. We didn't advertise our situation after what we'd just been through, but it must have been pretty clear. My parents being known there helped, but we're sure the big city is no place to bring up Nicky. Explaining to Nicky about why Rhona and I don't live together any more is more difficult than talking to him about his two mummies. He got used to that, but he keeps asking when will he, Rhona and I live together again. As I am still a regular part of his life, he can't understand why I have to live somewhere else. The effect of separation or divorce on the kids is the same whatever your sexuality, I suppose.

The HIV/AIDS epidemic has hit all communities, but in the UK the gay and lesbian community has been massively affected. Inevitably, the reality of people dying before their time because of AIDS is something lesbian and gay families are more likely to have to come to terms with.

Anne, 39, and Jenny, 41, mothers to Daniel, 10, and co-parent donor father, Roy, 38. *London*.

When Roy told us he was HIV-positive, my initial reaction was panic for me and our son, as well as tears of sadness for Roy. My personal fear wasn't logical, because Roy had undergone HIV tests before we started using his sperm donations. In fact, he'd had two HIV tests a few months apart, and had promised us he'd done nothing unsafe in the interim period. But you can't help panicking when one of the people closest to you, whom you've had intimate contact with (albeit through a turkey-baster) tells you he's HIV-positive. I did go for an HIV test. Jenny and I thought it would be the sensible thing to do to set my mind at rest, even though we were pretty sure it would be negative, which it was. We decided not to alarm Daniel with our personal concerns, which was just as well as things turned out. Roy is still perfectly healthy, and we hope will be for decades to come. In keeping with our openness and honesty with Daniel about our family set-up, and at Roy's suggestion, we agreed to let him explain to Daniel about his HIV status, and what that might mean for the future. Daniel has coped with it very well, but we have all agreed to keep it within the family. There is so much prejudice and hysteria on the subject of AIDS that we felt our family and Daniel's school career would be better off if we didn't publicize that particular fact. Many young people have to deal with the illness or loss of a parent, and although it won't be for many, many years we hope, at least the honest and direct dealing with the facts now can allow us all to cope as best as we can with whatever the future holds. It has made us a tighter family unit, and Roy's involvement as a father and co-parent has increased since the diagnosis. We all wanted it that way.

It can be a difficult decision to explain a complicated, and perhaps frowned-upon, history to a child and your family, and in the case of a gay male couple who have a child from a surrogate mother, it is not an easy decision to make.

Jim, 38, single father to Hayley, 8, born to a surrogate mother. *Isle of Wight*.

I only told my family twelve months ago. Jack and I split up and I went up north and told them the truth, that Hayley was born from a surrogate mother and that Jack and I were gay. Quite a few bombshells.

I have eleven brothers and sisters and my confessions earned their respect and admiration. They couldn't have been more supportive. My eldest brother had me really worried. I dreaded telling him and his response was just 'Well I wish you'd told me sooner, because if you had I'd have treated Jack totally different. I just thought he was your mate.' And I thought, 'Oh, all those years wasted.' My mother had died when I was born and I deliberately haven't seen my father for many years, so I've just got my brothers and sisters. Hayley knows I've got a dad and she's met him, because my sisters will take her to see him. They have a different relationship with him, but I won't see him after the terrible childhood he gave me.

I think it's important for Hayley to meet all the different members of the family, and to know the truth. She knows that she's from a surrogate mother, and she knows about Jack and me being gay; I told her everything. She's eight now and has coped with the information with no problems at all. Over the years, ever since she was born, I'd always intended to tell her I was gay. So I've always told her about people's prejudices, belief systems, different religions; that some people don't like people because they're black or disabled or gay. I just slipped being gay in there with all the other prejudices. Hayley just said 'Oh, OK.' So as much as a seven-year-old can understand, she understood. We sat together and watched all the horror stories from the war and all the things that were done, why they were done; because some of the people were Jews and other people were gay; and to Hayley they are on a par. It's just one form of prejudice, just like some people have to suffer this because they are black. She has a black uncle, my sister's boyfriend is black, he comes from Jamaica, and has explained similar things to her. She's clear that there are all kinds of prejudice.

Hayley seems so grown up about things. When she's up in Yorkshire with her aunts and uncles and I speak to her on the phone, it's like talking to an adult. She amazes me; it just shows how dealing in truth at a level kids can understand is not a problem for them; secrecy and lying to kids is what causes the damage.

Hayley and I talk a lot about things, but she's never come to me and asked me any questions about being gay. I'd like to know what she feels about it, as opposed to what she thinks about it. She must have feelings. If someone asks her where her parents are she'll say 'Well my special dad's at home, and my other special dad, because I've got two daddies, is at home with his mum.' (Jack and I have split up and he is back living with his mother now.) She says she has two dads because she's a 'very special child', she was 'really wanted', she 'wasn't just an accident'. This is what she quite openly tells people. I explained what a surrogate mother was, as best as you can to a seven-year-old child and that her mum had decided to move on. It didn't mean that she didn't love Hayley, it just meant that she had moved on to do other things, because she knew that Jack and I would always look after her.

I think that the hardest thing to explain to Hayley is why Jack left. I decided to come out when we split up, because I didn't have any choice. I couldn't bottle it all up and not tell anyone what I was going through. So when Jack left, and there was no chance of him ever coming back, that left me in a very awkward situation, because I'd been living this lie. So I went to the family and I told them and got total support, which I wasn't expecting at all. Then when I came back home I was totally isolated, because Jack and I had deliberately kept ourselves to ourselves. I realized this was no good, but couldn't see a way out. One day the woman who lived opposite came and knocked on the door and asked if Hayley would like to come and help her do some baking. It just developed from there over a few weeks. I was penniless and isolated, and in a right state. I'd been out of work for twelve months. I wasn't even on the phone. I told this woman, Carrie, straight away that I am gay. The next night we sat down, Carrie and I talking, and we talked right through the night. I told her everything. A few days later I saw my next-door neighbour and I told her everything. Neither of them batted an eyelid. They thought it was great. Like watching a film or something.

I had to go back to work and I needed a childminder. Carrie said 'Go for it, I'll look after Hayley.' At first I was a bit wary. Carrie's got four sons, so how could she cope with another child? But they were wonderful and took Hayley and me into their family. Carrie and I are the best of friends now. There isn't anything that we don't talk about. I even ended up mediating between her and her husband. He feels a little threatened by my relationship with Carrie, because we are so close.

In some ways I do not like the set-up that's evolved, because I feel separated from Hayley, but I need to work. Carrie actually sleeps in my house with Hayley and takes care of her during the week while I'm away with work. Carrie is the female role in Hayley's life. I'm quite happy about that part. Carrie's a wonderful person and she's got no hang-ups. She's not afraid to talk about anything. I'm away four nights a week, so Carrie picks Hayley up from school and they come home to my place so that Hayley's in her own environment. It's an escape for Carrie too, from a house with four males; she can watch what she wants to on television and she can keep an eye on her own house too, through the window. If Hayley had to sleep over there, I don't think it would work. I don't think we would cope with it, but because she's in her own home every night she's quite happy. She keeps telling everybody that I go on holiday every week. She can't see it as work and I always bring her something back, which she looks forward to.

The future's all up in the air at the moment. Jack used to visit once a week, but we cut it down to once a fortnight. I couldn't cope with it; Hayley and Jack coped. They were carrying on like nothing had changed. But I couldn't handle it. On his last visit I said that I'd prefer it if he either moved back in or moved out completely. I couldn't handle this in-between thing. One week he didn't turn up and I had hell from Hayley all week, that was really bad. She was so upset because he didn't come, and she said it was my fault. Then sometimes he wouldn't phone on time. I just couldn't handle it. He tells me he still loves me, but how can he move out and still feel that way? A few months ago he dropped a few papers through the letterbox about work. That was the last time I heard from him.

Hayley still asks about him all the time: When is he coming to visit? When is he going to ring? Slowly, she's getting the idea that he may not. I tell her that I can't answer for Daddy Jack. He must do what he thinks is right. Perhaps Jack feels that it would be better if we don't see each other for a while, and that we give ourselves time to settle down and get into a routine. Hayley seems to be accepting it, although Carrie tells me she still asks about him. I still often say 'Jack and I' even though he's gone, then I correct myself. Well, after twelve years together it's understandable, and for Hayley it's all she's ever known in her life, Daddy Jim and Daddy Jack. It's hard for us both at times.

What finally made him leave were two things. We were living such a lie; we had made up so many stories about how we'd got Hayley and who we were that we couldn't remember who we'd told what. That puts a real stress on a relationship. It wasn't until Jack left that I started living an honest life; what a relief. The other catalyst was that Jack's father died. His mother had been totally against him being with me. She had rung up for ten years saying, 'Why don't you come home and you'll get over this gay thing'. When his father died it really threw him off balance. His mother rang up every day, crying, 'I need you, I want you to come home.' After three months he gave in and went back. He was crying the night before, wouldn't tell me why, and the next day he went back to his mum. He left here in tears, telling me he'll never love anybody else. Once he'd moved back he was still acting like he lived here and I couldn't handle that. He'd keep dropping in, but not staying the night. He was working and I wasn't. He'd been our breadwinner and he'd pulled out. He didn't sort of say, 'Well I'll keep supporting you until you're in work.' He just sort of said, 'I'm off.' Thanks Jack; thank you, Jack's mum!

Notes

1. Lesbian and Gay Pride, the UK's annual celebration of lesbian, gay and bisexual pride that takes place in London in June or July; it includes a march of hundreds of thousands of lesbian and gay people and their friends and families through the centre of London, followed by the largest free festival in Europe, including live performances from some of the top names in the pop music world. It was renamed Lesbian, Gay, Bisexual and Transgender Pride for the 1996 event. In many other countries the equivalent event is called 'Christopher Street Day', after the street on which the Stonewall riots happened.

ELEVEN

School Days

Since the arrival of Clause 28 of the Local Government Act 1988, local authorities have been prohibited from doing anything that will 'intentionally promote homosexuality or publish material with the intention of promoting homosexuality'. Schools are further singled out by a prohibition on any activities which 'promote the teaching in any maintained school of the acceptability of homosexuality as a pretended family relationship'. This causes problems for many teachers in the addressing of homosexuality as a phenomenon, and can cause difficulties in teaching pupils to accept and understand classmates who have lesbian or gay parents, or who may be gay or lesbian themselves. Many teachers see the legislation as irrelevant and nonsensical.

Billie, 38, who co-parents her son Jamie, 7, with her partner Simone, 36, the donor father Mike, 36, and his partner, Mehmet, 31. *London.*

We all love going to school as the mums or dads. Well, we all dress like 'man or woman at C & A' because of our jobs, and the four of us are interchangeable as parents. It wasn't deliberate, but with us arriving at the school gates in every combination of ones, twos, threes or fours to collect Jamie, I think they all thought our household was some weird *ménage à quatre*. All the other parents were very friendly . . . jealous probably, or hoping for an invitation to dinner!

Terry, 36, teacher and donor father. *London.*

I teach my classes about homosexuality. They all know it exists anyway, and I am no more promoting homosexuality to them by teaching them about it truthfully, than I am promoting cannibalism to them by producing Sweeney Todd as the school play. It just doesn't hold water, intellectually, to ban the 'promotion of homosexuality' by outlawing teachers from discussing it in class. But I'm lucky. I work in an enlightened school, and I know the facts about being gay. There are many teachers out there who block any discussion of homosexuality because of fear of the law, pressure from their governors or because of ignorance. I'd hate to be a kid in one of their classes who's being bullied because of my queer parents. Where would they start?'

Some teachers just don't have the professional or personal opportunities to be able to tackle what can seem like a single-handed battle.

Lynn, 24, teacher. *North Wales.*

I'm not out at work, and I can't imagine being out in the school I'm in at the moment. It's a church school and the governors are very strict about sex education, especially abortion and homosexuality. I'm a form tutor, and one kid in my class was being picked on and teased quite badly by a lot of the others because his dad had left home . . . for another man. I heard from other teachers that this boy was being called 'queer' in the playground, and 'your dad's a poof'. Some of them started calling him 'Davida'. I made all the right noises; shouting at them, giving them detentions, making sure he wasn't harmed physically and they eased off on him a bit. But I couldn't bring myself to discuss the whole issue of homosexuality with the class. I wanted to tell them it's OK, it's normal, it's nothing to be ashamed of and to dispel some of the myths. But I couldn't. I was worried I would get into trouble with the head or the governors, worried they might start asking or gossiping about me, and I wasn't about to tell them about me. My head of department said the kids'd soon forget about David's dad and find some other scapegoat, which they did eventually, but it never went away completely. He was an easy target for some of the kids, but he also had a good circle of friends who stood by him and for whom it didn't matter. He also seemed quite a happy child,[1] but I never personally spoke to him about his father.

With these sort of dilemmas facing teachers, it's understandable that lesbian and gay parents take a range of different decisions about how open to be at school about their family situation. Here are a range of common attitudes to facing up to schooldays as lesbian or gay parents.

Lorraine, 39, and Rachel, 46, are mothers to Sarah, 13. *Manchester*.

Although we'd never come out to Sarah's friends and teachers at school, we knew they knew about us and it didn't seem to be a problem. I mean, how many of the other kids have two mums who both turn up to parents evenings, sports days and to collect their kid from school? But it made a big difference when they knew for sure. Eventually, I told a few of the other parents and teachers; the ones I knew could handle it. One of them asked me directly if Rachel and I were a couple, and I wasn't going to lie. Sooner or later some of Sarah's friends stopped coming round, and other parents stopped being friendly to us. Some of them stood around at the school gates talking about us and not even saying hello. The rest were the same to us as they'd always been, but it wasn't a nice atmosphere. Thank God it was Sarah's last year at primary school. We made sure she went to a secondary school miles away the following year, so she could make a fresh start. And we didn't make the same mistake at the new school.

One of the main myths that is trotted out to oppose lesbians and gays as parents is that their children will be mercilessly teased, ridiculed and bullied at school by peers, and possibly by staff, and that this would persist as a destabilizing force for life. In practice, young adults raised in lesbian families are no more likely to remember general teasing or bullying than those from heterosexual single-parent homes.[2] For those who do experience hostility from peers, there is no difference in how seriously they view the episodes. Although the children of lesbian and gay parents are more likely to be teased about their possible sexuality than children of heterosexual parents, there is no difference from the proportion of teasing that children of single-parent heterosexual families receive. It should also be reiterated here that no significant difference seems to exist in the sexual attraction to their own gender of young adults raised by lesbian or single heterosexual parents.[2]

Kirk, 37, whose partner Keith, 43, is the natural father to Kelly, 15, and Stuart, 18. *Leeds*.

When Kelly and Stuart came to live with us, we spent a lot of time choosing the right schools for them. We made a point of speaking at length to the headteacher, and were very clear about our status as gay parents and demanded that the school watched over the kids and looked for signs of bullying. We also said we'd expect the same non-tolerance of homophobic comments or prejudice against our kids as they would show to racist abuse in the school. To their credit, all the headteachers we saw were very positive and supportive of our requests. In the end we decided to send Kelly to a local junior school with a very multicultural range of pupils and a few children of lesbian parents. There was such diversity that she experienced little problem. For Stuart, things were a little more difficult. He was ready for secondary school and the local one was a very large school with a very male-dominated macho climate. He'd just come from a small-town, predominantly white school, and he wouldn't have coped well in that school. I went there for two days and sat in on lessons observing and saw that it was not the school for him. In the end we found a much smaller school with a female headteacher who was incredibly understanding, and she also spotted the possibility of Stuart having special needs. When we went to a meeting early on with some of the staff, I realized I recognized two of the female teachers, having seen them in one of the gay clubs in town. We smiled at each other across the room, but I didn't let on. It turned out to be a great place for Stuart to go to school from a pastoral point of view, as the two lesbian teachers kept an eye on him throughout his school career. When Kelly was ready for secondary school we were equally careful about the choice, and decided on an all-girls school.

They have both experienced problems at school because of our sexuality, so we were very glad that we had pre-empted these incidents in our initial talks with the headteachers. In Kelly's case she was verbally abused on only two occasions about us. She was very well-supported by the head of year and by her peers, who literally became her bodyguards to show the bullies whose side they were on and to protect Kelly. They didn't question Kelly's sexuality but were bad mouthing Keith and me to get at Kelly. It should be said that a lot of children in Kelly's school (and perhaps in all schools) are bullied and the two incidents that Kelly experienced actually mean she had a remarkably problem-free schooling, despite it being common know-ledge in the school that her dads were gay. Her confidence and self-respect didn't make her an easy target or allow her to take their ignorance too seriously. Stuart, in his first year at secondary school, had a number of incidents to deal with. He is quite a big lad and so his first reaction was to try to beat up the people who'd called him names. They were calling me and Keith names and were also saying that Stuart was probably a poof too. As it happens, both Kelly and Stuart appear to be heterosexual, not that their sexuality is an issue for us. Stuart lost the fights that he'd started and we had to talk him through more constructive ways of responding. First we explained to both of them that they didn't have to protect us. We are quite capable of looking after ourselves and they don't need to endanger themselves for a few empty words. Second, that if they are accused of being gay, they should explain that, as it happens, they're not, but what would it matter if they were; mature, intelligent people don't have a problem with it. Third, to feel free to get someone else to deal with it. It is fine to say to one of the supportive teachers, 'I can't deal with this. Can you sort it out please?' That is a position of strength and maturity, not cowardice. All of these strategies seemed to help and they both had very happy and fulfilling school careers. In fact, Kelly is a very popular young woman, she's had boyfriends since she was thirteen and is involved in the Air Training Corps. An interest in uniforms, eh?

Daniel, 32, separated from his wife Bridget, 31, and two daughters Ruth, 6, and Mary, 4. *Aberdeen.*

Ruth goes to a traditional school, and there are fewer unconventional families in that area. The school were informed that Bridget and I live separately and that I do co-parent. However, it is not relevant to tell them of my sexuality. Ruth doesn't know and I don't know if she ever will. Maybe one day she will get teased about us being separated, but I can't imagine anyone at school knowing I'm gay. If it happens, we'll have to deal with it, but so far she's happy and popular at school and I see no reason for that to change.

Sally, 26, with her lover Jan, 28, are mothers to Lucy, 2. *Manchester.*

Initially we wanted Lucy to go to the local school, but then we found out that you have to be Church of England, so we started going to church to satisfy them. Then we found out that you have to be married, and you have to be able to prove it to them. So we're thinking of home tutoring now. We have an obligation to educate our child, but we can do this at home or send her to school. We realize she might outstretch us, in which case she'd have to go to school or have a tutor. She's nearly three and currently we're teaching her things and making a happy environment for her. She knows all her numbers and letters already, and I don't want her to sit through her first year at school doing nothing, waiting for the others to catch up. If she wants to go to school when she's older, then she'll go to school. She knows what she wants, she's very clever.

Simon, 38, and his lover Giles, 43, with Nita, 37, and Cheryl, 39, are co-parents to James, 8, and Edward, 6. *Kent.*

A lot of children, not only at their school, but children that they know, come from other than conventional homes; broken homes, some have single parents, and mixed-race homes, and so on. So the notion of this ideal, this ordinary family, is a little exotic. So perhaps that mitigates the potential problems that we might have. The schools know our menage, as it were . . . that there are four parents and two households, that the two mothers live together. It was inevitable that the schools would know all the parents. The mothers are there every day, and my partner and I do go there for concerts and things like that. I don't know that they made anything of that, but I think they may have just thought for a minute. It may have been that living in the sort of rural area in which the two women live, they would perhaps not have put two and two together, because it wouldn't have occurred to them. The women haven't expressly gone and told the school of the actual set-up, but haven't hidden the fact that they are co-parenting together. I think that they've not seen it as necessary to make any particular statement. After all, when children are involved, you've got to be very careful about exposing them to attitudes over which they have no control. But in fact, there's been no sense of having to be very covert. Having said that, of course, every gay person knows that there may be some ways in which we live our lives covertly, without even knowing that. So they might have taken unconscious steps to conceal their tracks as it were. I don't know. I don't think that they even know themselves. The boys' classmates, I think, are a little young at the moment to be hostile or fully aware. The classmates that have been aware, the kids that come to play with them, and come to birthday parties, seem to have no problem with us. Parents of children come as well, and they know what the situation is, and in some cases they've become friends. Children of colleagues have come to the house too. But there's been no adverse comments made so far. Of course, this might happen and no doubt will happen in the future.

Graham, 47, father to Yvonne, 27. *London and Yorkshire.*

I wasn't really involved with school, because my partner and I lived in London and my daughter, Yvonne, lived in Yorkshire. She came to see us in London and thought that it was wonderful, and wanted to come and live with me and Mick. She thought London was the best place on earth (I would agree with her to some extent). My ex-wife realized that Yvonne wasn't getting on with her new husband, Yvonne's new stepfather. So Yvonne asked if she could come and live with me and Mick in London. But I said it wouldn't be a good idea, because it would depend on catchment areas for the school, and the school in the area wasn't very nice. My real reason was that I think that it would have been a baptism of fire, coming from Yorkshire and going to a tough school in London. She was in the middle of O-levels at school and I thought it would be much too disruptive.

Maggie, 36, and Shelley, 40, mothers to twins, 4. *London.*

One of the interesting things is that you come up against more institutions. Where we were living before, we had a doctor who was all right about it and treated us like a normal family; there wasn't an issue about us being lesbians. But when you come up against schools, you realize, for all the best will in the world, they are definitely not sensitive environments to differences in families. For example, they send the kids home with Mother's Day cards, and yes we've got two kids, so we got two cards, but I wonder if we didn't have two kids whether we would have got two cards. I suspect we wouldn't at all. Since they have been at school, the kids have come back with this huge fantasy world about mummies and daddies. Every single night, in bed, one of the toys is a mummy and one of the toys is a daddy, and one of them is a big sister. They've got this huge, rich fantasy world all about a 'normal', heterosexual family that's only come from school, can only have come from school, hasn't come from us, hasn't come from their friends, hasn't come from nanny. It's simply come from school, and it's extraordinary, solid, fixed in their brains, that there are mummies and daddies and there are big sisters and brothers. That's what they live out in their fantasy life entirely, and they take turns at being mummies and daddies, every now and again with their 'children'.

In a way I find that more understandable because it's in an average school, where the majority are going to be children of heterosexual families, but there are other children of lesbian and gay families in that school. There is always something that you are going to come up against and most of it you know when you set out. But we didn't know that it was going to be constant. We didn't know that it was going to be all day, every day, from everybody, and the children too, not that the kids do it intentionally. We just didn't realize that every single minute, of every single day, the minute that you talk about anything to do with the children, and the minute that the children talk about anything to do with their family, it becomes an issue.

Jim, 38, single father to Hayley, 8, born to a surrogate mother. *Isle of Wight.*

One thing that Jack and I did hide from Hayley until she was seven was that we were gay. I was terrified of how she would cope with that at school. The worst moment was about four months ago, coming home from school. She wouldn't talk about it, but I knew something was bothering her. One child had stood up in school and had said, 'My parents are gay.' The teacher got very cross and angry with this little boy and this frightened Hayley, because she knew her parents were gay. She didn't know how to deal with it. I went to see the teacher, who told me that she had become angry because, 'He shouldn't have shouted it out in front of all the other children.' She felt he could have opened himself up to victimization and so she didn't want to give it any serious attention. But Hayley didn't understand this until we explained it to her, and said that some things are best not said, unless to your best friends, or your teacher. She was quite happy about that. The teacher has agreed to cover the topic more fully too.

Pam, 40, now separated from Rhona, 25, and their son, Nicky, 6. *Bristol.*

Now we live in the countryside, and after our bad experiences with anti-lesbian abuse and violence when we lived in Bristol, we decided to keep quiet about our situation with Nicky's school. It wasn't all bad in Bristol though; the nursery spotted us as a lesbian couple and were great about it. They made sure they talked about mummy and Pam when they discussed families and home life with Nicky, rather than just the traditional mummies-and-daddies picture of things. I felt really included. Out in the country here it's such a small community and people were so welcoming that we thought we'd leave people to guess. What they don't know can't hurt them . . . or (after the violence we got in the city) us!

Notes

1. See discussion on effect of peer-group hostility on children of lesbian and gay parents in this chapter, p. 108ff.

2. S. Golombok and F. Tasker (1995) Adults raised as children in lesbian families. *American Journal of Orthopsychiatry*, 65(2): 203–15.

TWELVE

It's a Difficult Age

Many parents dread the arrival of their children's teenage years. Difficult communication, irrational behaviour and dabbling with the habits, substances and behaviour of the adult world, before they are fully competent or mature to handle them, are all nightmares that parents frequently have of their kids as teenagers. Add to the usual 'coming of age' traumas the presence of homosexual parents, and one can see how an easily embarrassed or deeply conformist (within his or her peer group) teenager might rebel even more against this injustice or unnecessary burden, as they see it. In reality, though, have the parents of lesbian and gay teenagers found much hostility to their homosexuality?[1]

Yvonne, 27, daughter of gay father Graham, 47. *Yorkshire.*

I was aware of my dad's relationship. He talked about it as a gay relationship, and Mick as his partner. As a teenager, when I got to know him again when he came home from abroad, I never asked any questions or wanted any intimate details or anything. I'd have liked to know, but when he wanted to talk to me about anything, about me or him, I blocked it. I'm not a very open person about emotions or motivations. I don't have any problems about it deep down, but as a teenager I was very embarrassed about it. Especially as he arrived in my life so late. Had I grown up knowing him and his situation, then it would have been common currency when I was an awkward teenager. It's really important to tell kids the truth early on and let them accept it as their normal situation, then the problems get into perspective. It's all out in the open and much healthier. I'm a mother now, of two kids, from two different men. One was my first husband's child, and my second baby is with my new partner, but he and I aren't married. My dad and I aren't very close really, but he loves my kids, and I can't help thinking, when I see him with them, that they are getting honesty, attention and time with him that I never had.

Kirk, 37, whose partner Keith, 43, is the natural father to Kelly, 15, and Stuart, 18. *Leeds*.

The kids knew Keith and I were a gay couple long before they were teenagers, so it wasn't fresh ammunition for them as teenagers. In fact, it's fair to say it's never been used against us systematically; yes, there have been occasional comments in the heat of a teenage tantrum, but they are actually very protective of us and have defended our 'honour' verbally and physically at school. Kelly has had only two incidents in her secondary school career and Stuart slightly more, but they certainly aren't hung up on the fact of our sexuality, nor does it dominate our lives together in any significant way. It is incidental, and the teenage flash points are relatively few, and not centred on their dads being gay.

At times it was particularly difficult for Kelly, being brought up by two men. Her mother couldn't cope with her and her brother so they came to live with me and Keith, at very short notice, seven years ago. Unfortunately, Kelly's mother told her they had to go and live with their father and me because the schools are better round here. So perhaps it's not surprising that in moments of anger as a teenager she's said things like, 'I want my mother', 'You don't love me' and 'I want to go back and live with my mother'. In fact, her mother still causes conflict and upset for the kids, because she sometimes promises to visit and doesn't turn up, or birthdays and Christmas will pass without a card, present or phone call from her. Kelly particularly gets upset when these things happen. We did try to make sure that there were adult female role models around for Kelly and, in particular, a friend of ours became Kelly's 'Auntie Jay' and would call round often and take Kelly out sometimes. One part of growing up Keith and I panicked about was how to tackle Kelly's education and introduction to menstruation. Keith called Boots the Chemist's head office and was eventually passed on to yet another woman, this time in the science lab. She cottoned on to what the situation was, and the next day a huge parcel arrived containing every description of sanitary towel and tampon, plus loads of leaflets; all free. We talked through it all with Kelly, and then one day I noticed that some of the sanitary towels had been taken. So I asked Kelly if she'd started menstruating. She told me she hadn't, but she was wearing sanitary towels in her knickers once in a while to get used to them and the feel of it. So I think we did a pretty good job of preparing her without embarrassment.

Bert, 59, father to two adult sons and grandfather to one grandchild.
Surrey.

I regret that my children had to go through the trauma of a broken home, and that they had warring parents. However, after leaving my marriage and the family home and coming out to myself, I became much more understanding and accepting of them, and consequently their teenage years were a very pleasant time for us. I really enjoyed my kids as teenagers, although I didn't come out to them until they were in their early twenties and late teens respectively. I was very worried about coming out to my sons so I phoned a radio problems phone-in programme. They were very helpful, and said that if I had a good relationship with my sons they would probably accept it pretty well. So I told my eldest son, and he was slightly surprised and was quiet for a few moments. Then you could see all sorts of things clicked for him and he had loads of questions. He was very interested in my life and has met quite a few of my gay friends. He is straight himself and is now divorced with one son, but he is not homophobic in any way. I didn't tell my younger son at the same time, and shortly after telling my elder son, the younger one was looking after my house while I was away and found a copy of *Gay Times*. He immediately called his elder brother and wanted to know what was going on. Not the ideal way to come out to your son, but he's also fine about it and has no problem telling his friends that his dad's gay. He has also been married and divorced.

Lorraine, 39, and Rachel, 46, are mothers to Sarah, 13. *Manchester.*

Our daughter is only thirteen, but she's already got an eighteen-year-old boyfriend. That freaked us out a bit. After all, we suspected he wanted sex; what else does an eighteen-year-old want with a thirteen-year-old? The last thing we wanted was to create a confrontation or to forbid her from seeing him. We didn't want to demonize sex or to drive it underground. She's always been very open with us about things, we've fostered that atmosphere. So, we encouraged them both to register with a youth health centre that gives advice and 'supplies'. We talked to her about non-penetrative sex as a starting point, rather than assuming intercourse was the only option. We also talked about contraception. We made sure we advocated that sex is a good and pleasurable thing.

Too many people of all sexualities are inhibited or ashamed about sex. But we also stressed that with sex comes a responsibility, and that contraception is top priority, as is safer-sex awareness. One of our neighbours has an eighteen-year-old daughter who is about to have her third child. Sarah thinks that would be a nightmare situation for her to be in. But as far as us being queer being a focus of teenage rebellion and dissatisfaction . . . er . . . no, not in our house. It's an old story, and there's little mileage to be got out of beating us with that stick. She's got to find better missiles than that to get us going, so she doesn't bother with it.

Stephen, 48, and his lover Gerry, 43, are co-parents to Jack, 18, and Edwin, 16. *Cambridge*.

When I was a child I was a very awkward little bugger, and I used every bit of ammunition I could in fighting with my siblings and my parents. My eldest son takes after me. The younger one is much sunnier-natured, he's a very jolly kid. But we have had problems. There's bound to be difficulties, in the teenage years particularly, with any family, not just with lesbian and gay parents. I remember being deeply embarrassed about my very reasonable, middle-class parents, who were not in the least bit outrageous or unusual. I've been embarrassed by them on numerous occasions. I think children almost always are. Now how much more embarrassing must your parents be at this stage in life if your parent is perceived as being peculiar, in ways which might not be approved by society? Particularly if you are in that sort of conformist stage, which I think we all go through. My sons' teenage years, which frequently throw up difficulties anyway for families, have been exacerbated by the problems of other people's reactions to our sexuality. Both of our sons appear to be heterosexual, and they have certainly called us a few names in the heat of an argument. It's certainly not something I think dominates their relationship with us, and we are certainly a loving and supportive family unit. Our eldest son has recently gone off to university, and we will no doubt see a reduction in the few small examples of embarrassment or shame he shows occasionally. Our younger son seems very flippant about it all and has experienced very little difficulty at school or with friends about us. It depends how much importance you attach to people's comments. Our elder son interprets it as a reflection on him, our younger son sees it as a comment on us and he is protective of us, but ultimately doesn't see it as people's view of his sexuality. But I don't want to give a false picture; these moments are tiny parts of a full, rich interaction between us and our sons on all levels of life. Our kids have a very strong, well-balanced, loving home; they are extremely materially secure, and benefit from our set-up in all sorts of ways. And I think this will come through to them, especially our elder son, eventually.

Graham, 47, father to Yvonne, 27. *London and Yorkshire.*

I felt very sad that I couldn't do more for my daughter, that she was having problems with her stepfather. There was one time when she was appealing to me to take her in. My first reaction was to do so, but being more objective about it, I realized that it would possibly lead to even more problems than she was leaving behind. We had a small house in those days, it just wasn't feasible on lots of levels. Her mother actually wanted me to take her in. Funnily enough, living with my gay partner wasn't the main issue, not an issue at all really. For my daughter or my ex-wife. My daughter's never asked me anything about me and Mick. When she first came down to London, and I had been living with my partner for eighteen months, she came to stay with us for a month. Very early on she said, 'Do you sleep with him in there?', as we passed my bedroom, and I said, 'Yes'. She gave one of her stock teenage responses 'Oh,' and that was it really. We didn't communicate very well really. I was having to form a relationship with a new young adult then, whom I hadn't actually seen for two years as I'd been abroad. There had been letters and birthday and Christmas presents, but now she was no longer a young girl. She was a young woman.

Notes

1. For a discussion of the research findings that show children of homosexual parents are no more likely to suffer from teasing or from painful recollection of incidents than children of heterosexual single-parent families, see Chapter 11.

THIRTEEN

Free at Last

For lesbian and gay parents who have had their custody challenged, their child's sixteenth birthday is a milestone that they greet with open arms. One of the most frequent fears of parents of any persuasion is that they will lose their children. For that to be a distinct possibility, motivated by prejudice, ignorance, the collapse of a heterosexual marriage or some of the other reasons recounted in Chapter nine, means that for many parents they do not feel secure as parents until their children are no longer minors. It is an issue particularly strongly felt by lesbian and gay parents, who know only too well how hostile attitudes in a heterosexual society can all too easily threaten one's family. So what does it actually mean to lesbian and gay households when your child finally becomes sixteen, and you no longer have to look over your shoulder?

Once your child becomes an adult, other questions become more prominent too, like, 'What is the sexuality of my child?' One might expect most lesbian or gay parents to be stoically indifferent to the sexuality of their sons and daughters, particularly as such a big deal was probably made of their own sexuality; one might expect an attitude of total acceptance – no matter what. This is often, but not always, the case, and usually depends on how accepting the parent is of his or her own sexuality, as some of these stories also show. (See also 'Gwen's' story in Chapter 14.)

Wendy, 40, mother to Natasha, 13, whom she co-parents with Penny, 38. *West Midlands*.

My daughter is thirteen and I dream of the day she turns sixteen and I can forget the threat, admittedly now only a threat on paper, that my custody of her can still be challenged. When she was seven, I won custody as an out lesbian of my daughter, in dispute with my ex-husband. This decision was overturned on appeal, and custody was given to my ex-husband because the judge said my daughter would be better off in a 'conventional household'. The High Court ruled that my lesbian relationship didn't mean I couldn't be a good mother, and she was returned to me. That was five and a half years ago. After a nightmare like that lasting eighteen months, I'm not surprised I'm counting the days until it can never happen again. I've tried to play it down for my daughter's sake. She was very insecure for years about whether she would be moved again. Her sixteenth birthday is going to be one hell of a celebration!

Rachel, 51, and Bette, 48, mothers to two adult daughters. *Cheshire.*

We're the oldest lesbian parents we know of, and that's not just because we live in Cheshire, which isn't exactly a hotbed of lesbian colonization. We know women couples in many parts of the country, and none of them know older lesbian mothers either. Of course, there are much older lesbian mothers around, but they're very well-hidden, even now. It was incredibly radical of us in the late 1960s and early 1970s to decide to live together and bring up my two children from my failed marriage. We were just lucky that my ex-husband was such an unreliable so-and-so, and there was no way he would want to keep the children or that he could provide a stable, bread-winning environment for them. I can't imagine we would have won a custody battle in those days. I had fears for many years that one day it would all come out, and we'd have to be judged and probably lose the children. We were very careful at school, with neighbours and some friends, to make sure we gave the impression of being best friends, very sisterly, rather than lovers. We lived in a smallish cottage for many years, with only two bedrooms, which made for far fewer questions from our daughters. All they had ever known was to share a room and so for their mother and Bette to do the same was not unusual. When the second of our girls reached sixteen we did feel as if a great weight had been lifted off our shoulders. The girls were delighted we made such a big occasion of their sixteenth birthdays, and they put it down to us having lived through the 1960s and still seeing teenage years as really significant. We didn't disabuse them of that idea; well, it also made us seem a bit more with-it than the image they usually have of us. By the time the girls were sixteen I'm sure it would have been very difficult to take them away from us anyway, as we could have shown what a good upbringing they'd had and that to take them away from us after so many years would be much more damaging than any of the alarmist thoughts bigots might have (but couldn't prove). When you've lived with a fear for so many years, and censored yourselves on so many levels, it's very difficult to suddenly drop those habits. Our daughters gradually came to realize the extent of the 'friendship' between Bette and me. Yes, there were the occasional ugly moments during teenage years, when they were grappling with the shame and confusion they felt about coming from a different family, but now they are so happy, secure and uninhibited about their lives and desires. Both of them had boyfriends as youngsters, and our eldest daughter is married and is a mother. Our younger daughter is single at the moment, and she doesn't rule out the possibility of having a same-sex friendship, but we think she's just being polite and kind; she's as straight as anything. She's just very broadminded, which is a relief to us after all the covering up we did, although most of that was outside of the family home. We were open in discussions of feelings and the acceptance of difference and of homosexuality, even though we didn't necessarily spell out the intimate details of my and Bette's relationship. The roles are very much reversed now, and the hidden rebels we felt ourselves to be in the 1960s and 1970s are now viewed by our daughters as rather conservative and secretive still. I don't think we're that cagey any more, but our daughters, particularly the younger one, often say to us when we use a euphemism or laugh off a personal question, 'God, mum, you haven't still got things in your closet, have you?' We did it for them, and now they're very good for us.

Stephen, 48, and his lover Gerry, 43, are co-parents to Jack, 18, and Edwin, 16. *Cambridge*.

My own experience of being gay has been an extremely positive one. Being gay has meant that I simply do not have available to me that sort of dull suburban conformity which is almost foisted upon most people. My life is extremely enjoyable. Lots of possibilities are open to me that would not have been had I been heterosexual. It meant, for instance, that I have had children at a later stage of my life, and therefore I am materially better-off than I might have been if I had gone into it as a twenty-two-year-old. If all of those things are available to my children, I think that it would be good for them to be gay. I should also say that because of the profession I'm in, and because of the social group I am in, I experience very little, practically no, prejudice in my life, and my family have always been pretty good. But of course, you can't imagine that that would be the same for everybody.

There is a real sense of peace and satisfaction now the boys are both over sixteen. Not that we have had any custody worries in reality. When Gerry's wife died when the boys were small, there was never any doubt about his custody, although when he and I started living together a year and a half later a few of his widow's relatives raised eyebrows, but were far too hung up and polite to do anything about it, and also knew, loved and trusted Gerry with his sons. I have had irrational worries about the social services just turning up at the door one day, out of the blue, with poisonous rumours about two gay men and their young sons. I know there are such stupid myths in people's minds about gay men and kids, when in fact it is heterosexual men, usually fathers or straight relatives, who perpetrate virtually all child abuse.* Occasionally you hear stories of parents being visited by the social services with malicious or mis-interpreted rumours from neighbours, colleagues or teachers. Once in a while, while the boys were under sixteen, I realized how easy it would have been for any homophobic individual to have torn our family apart. These irrational nightmares evaporate when the kids are old enough.

You also come through to a more mature relationship with your kids and they begin to appreciate the benefits of a really open, honest upbringing, where the truth about ourselves, the world and sexuality has been common currency. It is gratifying to see two well-adjusted young men going out into the world able to discuss and deal with issues and aspects of life so many of their peers are unduly embarrassed or inhibited about. The ability to talk openly about your emotions and about intimate aspects of life is a liberating way to be. I think we've done well by them.

Both of our sons appear to be heterosexual, but I'd be quite indifferent in a way as to whether they ultimately turn out gay or not.

---

*The commonly held belief is that children are more at risk of abuse by homosexual men than by heterosexual men. There is no evidence for this, nor is there any evidence of paedophilia being linked to homosexuality. In fact, it appears to be much more closely allied to incest, a predominantly heterosexual domain.[1,2] Very often the same man who abuses children will abuse children of both sexes and adult women too.[3] Children are just as much at risk of sexual assault by a heterosexual parent or step-parent as by a homosexual counterpart. There is very little evidence of any significant occurrence of child sexual abuse by women, including lesbian women.[4]

I'd be much more concerned about whether they turned out to be Tories or racists or something like that. I do have a sort of thought, and this is going to sound terrible, that if they are heterosexual the chances of my having grandchildren are that much greater, and perhaps that might be a good thing. But then again, so many heterosexuals end up having kids automatically or because it's an expectation, rather than lesbian and gay parents, who so often have thought it all out so carefully, and planned thoroughly for the future. I started off in parenthood saying that I hadn't been very interested in being a father, and now I'm talking about the pleasurable prospect of being a grandfather. But when it comes down to it I don't mind what the sexuality of my sons is either way really.

John, now divorced, father to Gary, 11, and Emma, 10. *Hull*.

I would hope in all honesty that my kids grow up to be heterosexual, because life would be a lot easier for them. If they were bisexual or homosexual it wouldn't bother me in the slightest. I just think that any parent wants their child to be happy, and to have an easy life, and with society being generally homophobic, life would be a lot easier for them as heterosexuals. If I could press a button and be straight then I would. No question of that, I would. I'm not ashamed of being gay, although obviously that conflicts to some extent with what I've just said. And, I suppose, I'm a hypocrite on that one. I'm not sure. It's simply a question of having an easier life. Why make life more difficult by questions of sexuality? I can't say I was so proud of being straight when I was living a straight lifestyle. So why should I be proud, living a gay lifestyle? But if my kids do turn out gay, then so be it, they've obviously got someone here who knows a bit about it to support them.

Shelley, 40, and Maggie, 36, mothers to twins, 4. *London*.

It's silly, but I'll be glad when the twins are sixteen. A common phrase around here, not in the hearing of the children, because they repeat everything that we say, is that 'We'd better not do or say that, because if the social workers find out we'll be in trouble.' Now I mean, I think we live, in general terms, a very ordinary middle-of-the-road life. We've both got very boring jobs in, dare I say, local government. And we don't live to excess or have a wild life in any way at all. But there are odd little things that happen. I don't know, one of the kids puts on somebody else's clothes, like children do when they are dressing up perhaps, and we'll say we'd better not do that in front of someone who might tell the social workers; it's a joke, it's not meant seriously. But there is a sort of permanent consciousness that because we are going to be watched and scrutinized, that just normality isn't enough, we've got to be better than that, we've got to be squeaky clean. We get questioned a lot by people about our situation, and that's understandable, because I think it's just a reflection of where society's at. Acceptance of lesbians and gay men may be growing, but acceptance of them being part of families and having children is growing at such an incredibly small rate that it's going to take a long time before we see real progress. In that sense, people's inquisitiveness about us is understandable, but not in my view justifiable. It really is just a reflection of society's views of the perversion of lesbians and gay men. There's no way you can condone it. The older the kids get, the less worries I have of people talking, but I'll have some worries, I'm sure, until they're sixteen.

Once the children have reached adulthood, many lesbian and gay parents advocate total openness, if that wasn't in operation already, while others still exercise caution and do not disclose the facts outside the family home. Within the household it is usually impossible to have hidden the reality of a same-sex couple sharing a bedroom, but in some situations it is possible to shield the children from the facts about your sexuality completely. The following example from the child's view explains some of the reasons for and effects of total masking of the parent's sexuality.

Una, 28, daughter of gay father Jim, 63. *Essex.*

My father didn't come out until after my mother died, over six years ago. We had been going through a hard time since her death, and my dad was leading his own life and I mine, although I was still living at home. Things sort of got tense. He started acting a bit strangely to me, dressing a bit strangely. He was going out every night and coming back about four in the morning. You know, sort of coming in as if nothing had happened. And there were strange phone calls, and whispering on the phone. Something was going on, but I didn't know what. It took about two or three years before Dad actually said something. But already then, I had twigged. Well, all the phone calls were from men, there were no ladies, and Dad had sort of started resenting ladies, or sort of shutting them out. The only ladies he knew were Mum's old friends, and the way he was acting . . . I didn't like it. He wasn't the father that I knew, and loved and respected. In a way, it was frightening me. He came out to me because he had several counselling sessions. I thought he was going because he'd been recently widowed. Anyway, he came home one night, and said, 'Could you come to my next counselling session with me?' And I thought 'OK if it's going to help you . . .'. My realization was still in the back of my mind, but until you hear it you still have some doubts. In the days leading up to his next session we had several heated conversations, which just ended up in mighty rows, because Dad was so obviously denying everything and behaving so secretly. In the counselling session Dad just broke down and cried and said, 'I'm gay,' and I said, 'I know.' He just looked at me, and I said, 'Why didn't you tell me before? I knew.' At that moment I wanted to tell him the truth; that I was a lesbian, but I couldn't. Although in the back of my mind I was prepared to have him confirm that he was gay, actually I wasn't. I just felt numb. All I could do was sit down and comfort him and say, 'It's no problem. You're still my Dad,' and whatever. But when I actually came home, over the next few days, I was going over and over it in my mind, and I thought, 'Oh my gawd.' I had a girlfriend at the time and I went to see her and said to her, 'I don't know what to feel or do.' And she said, 'You're being a hypocrite.' We talked it through and I realized I was glad Dad had come out. It gave light at the end of the tunnel and he was able to speak to me more, to have more confidence in me. But I had this secret inside of me, and I didn't know how to tell him. It must seem odd to some people that there were two very closeted people, father and daughter, in the same family for so many years, and even when he came out to me I couldn't reciprocate. But it just wasn't done in our family, that sort of emotional, intimate conversation.

I finally told my dad about me being gay. I kept thinking, 'I've got to tell him,' but I couldn't bring myself to tell him verbally. So I wrote him a letter, and thinking about it now, I wish I hadn't, because it upset him more. The letter explained the situation and, as I was still living at home at the time, I left it on the breakfast table, before going to visit my brother in Shropshire for the day. When I got there, there was a message from Dad who had phoned to say 'everything was all right'. On the way home that evening I was more or less rehearsing what I was going to say to him. He wasn't home when I arrived, and I was very nervous, knowing he'd read the letter. He arrived home about an hour after I did, and he said he'd known years ago, before I did, and that really shocked me; that he'd known for years and said nothing. But even though he was now out and I had done likewise, he wouldn't accept my partner for a long time. He would grudgingly ask, 'Well how's so and so?', and I would say, 'Oh, she's fine, I'm going round to see her tonight . . .' 'Oh right', he would say. The first Christmas was a bit hard with this sort of atmosphere, but then, and I don't know how it happened, he just finally accepted her. They get on so well now. He actually said it's like having another daughter around, and he asks her round all the time. He's lovely to her, which is really good.

For me it was probably hard to accept my father's sexuality, because he was already married to Mum and they had had such a lovely married life. I couldn't understand why he was doing this. At the time, I suppose, I would have preferred him, and probably still now, to have found a lady friend, and get married. But obviously she wouldn't replace my mother. I would like my father to find someone, so that he'd be happy, and I wouldn't have to worry about him when he was old and retired and on his own; so that he would actually have company in his life. Even now he's still looking back to Mum. I can't do any more for him. From what I hear about him finding male partners, and what I hear about the various friends he's made, it's almost been a wrong decision for him. A couple of them I have met. They're very nice people. But others . . . I think he seems to get in the wrong crowd, and he doesn't realize until it's too late. There's a chap who lives with him now. I think he's very nice. But I still think he's taking Dad for a ride, basically, and I don't like to see that happening. I can't tell him . . . as long as he's happy. I just hope that he's happy but I still wish he could have a woman companion. I don't know why I say that. I suppose it's just society.

As far as I could see as a child, I thought he was totally heterosexual. He was just for Mum all the time. He did go out to his local gym a lot. When AIDS awareness programmes first came up years ago, and people were really worried about what was going to happen, Dad was really into it. In fact, he was very concerned about it, about how dangerous it was. I think he was worried about the future, and thinking in case I met someone, and how he thought things could be transmitted. He didn't see AIDS as primarily gay. He went and did more research about it. My mum and I used to laugh at him because he was so serious about it all, not in an unkind way, but to see that he was so engrossed in this subject. It was basically because we didn't understand what it was all about, and I didn't see any gay in him.

Notes

1. R. Langevin (1983) *Sexual Strands. Understanding and Treating Sexual Anomalies in Men*. London: Lawrence Erlbaum.
2. J. R. Conte (1991) The nature of sexual offences against children. In C. R. Hollen and K. Howells (eds), *Clinical Approaches to Sex Offenders and Their Victims*. Chichester: John Wiley, pp.11–34.
3. G. Abel, J. Becker, J.Cunningham-Rather, M. Mittleman and J. L. Rouleau (1988) Multiple paraphilic diagnoses among sex offenders. *Bulletin of American Academy of Psychiatry Law*, 16: 153–68.
4. D. Finkelhor and D. Russell (1984) Women as perpetrators: review of the evidence. In D. Finkelhor (ed.), *Child Sexual Abuse: New Theory and Research*. New York: Free Press, pp.171–87.

FOURTEEN

Too Many Grandmas

With more and more out lesbian and gay parents, it stands to reason that there are increasing numbers of out lesbian and gay grandparents. The likelihood is that the children of lesbian and gay parents are heterosexual,[1] and, consequently, granny or granddad being out may present some complications. The other possible difference from heterosexual families is that in the case of families with three or more co-parents, there may well be up to eight or more grandparents. How's that for innovation?! However, whether the grandparents are lesbian, gay or straight, there's no guarantee they will be totally approving of their offspring, or their offspring's offspring.[2]

Simon, 38, and his lover Giles, 43, with Nita, 37, and Cheryl, 39, are co-parents to James, 8, and Edward, 6. *Kent*.

All of our parents have been absolutely marvellous. There are six grandparents, mine, my partner's and Cheryl's. Nita has lost her parents. For Cheryl's mother and father, James is their only natural grandchild. But both they, my parents and my partner's parents have taken on not only their natural grandchild, but also our younger son, willingly and happily, with no distinction between the two boys whatsoever. All credit to my parents, who have plenty of other grandchildren, but that's the way they are. So there has been absolutely no problem at all. In fact, it sometimes feels like there are too many grandparents.

Gwen, 59, grandmother to Max, 1, and mother to Wendy, 30. *Liverpool*.

I feel quite mischievous, almost subversive, about my relationship with my grandson. Well, you see, I'm basically an old hippie, and it's a source of frustration to me that my daughter has turned out to be so conventional and conservative in her outlook. Maybe it was a reaction to my non-conformity during her upbringing, but I can't help feeling she would have a more exciting life if she was a little less conventional. She says she's really happy, and I believe her, but I want my grandson to have a *really* exciting life without all the expectations and conformity I know she'll be teaching him as he gets older. So, whenever I'm alone with him I make sure I start his proper education and broaden his horizons. I know it's only childish rebellion in me at the moment, because he doesn't understand a word I'm saying, but I do sing him things like 'Glad to Be Gay' and camp songs like 'Over the Rainbow'. I think it would be great if he grew up to be a dancer or a sculptor or something, and had fabulous arty boyfriends. I can just see his mother's face when they all come to my house for tea and I can say, 'Well, it does sometimes skip a generation.' My greatest fear is that he'll grow up to be an estate agent.

Graham, 47, father to Yvonne, 27. *London and Yorkshire.*

I have two grandchildren. They've got different fathers. I see them two or three times a year. I make it a point that we do see more of each other than I saw of my daughter, even though they live a long way away. My granddaughter's only five and my grandson's only two, so the question of my partnership, my relationship with my partner here, doesn't come into it.

I didn't have a lot of contact with my daughter as a father in her formative years, which is regrettable. I think my daughter is actually a little bit resentful that her children, and particularly her daughter, get a lot of attention from me. She's maybe thinking, 'Why didn't I get this?' I can tell that. People would say, 'How do you know?', but I can read body language, I can listen to comments made. We did have a break, an argument. There was a long silence about the time my grandson was born, but we made up again. When I suggest we should have a really good talk about it, about what happened . . . she just clams up.

I don't like being known as a gay father or a gay grandfather. I don't like being called a gay anything. I'm me, really. A gay friend once asked me to come to a dinner party, 'You'll be the token gay grandfather', he laughed. I really resented it, because I'm me first, and I'm all the things that make up me. I'm not a label. It's obviously going to be of interest to people, because it's quite unusual. I just think there's more to me than just one thing that makes up part of my life.

Billie, 38, who co-parents her son Jamie, 7, with her partner Simone, 36, the donor father Mike, 36, and his partner, Mehmet, 31. *London*.

We're not short of parents in our family. There's always someone around to hold the fort, so it gives us great flexibility. In fact, the problem is quite the opposite. Getting time with the kids can be a problem, for the men particularly. And then there's the thorny question of the grandparents. Mehmet's parents are out of the country, and Simone's lost her father, so we only have five to deal with. But they are all so enthusiastic, especially as for three of them it's their only grandchild, they spoil him rotten. Summer is the worst time for competing for Jamie. Honestly, that's what it feels like sometimes. We have to be quite strict with timetabling, and we identify weekends far in advance for visits, so that Jamie has some sort of stability and continuity of home life. But he loves it; being the centre of attention and having the freedom of umpteen different households. I don't think there's any doubt he knows he's wanted. That boy's not going to have any trouble being in company, that's for sure!

Beth, 63, grandmother to Tina, 6, and Tracey, 4, and mother to Douglas, 36. *Devon*.

My granddaughters love to come and visit us here in Devon, and once or twice a year we go up to Bedfordshire to visit them, but I can't help feeling that my son is uneasy every time we're left alone with the girls. Oh, it's not worries over their safety. He doesn't have any of those silly notions about lesbians and small girls. He knows that is ignorant rubbish. He grew up with us after all, I think he knows us well enough. But that's why he's uneasy. He knows Marjorie and I won't make a secret of our relationship, and he hasn't had the 'your grandmothers are rather special' conversation with the girls yet. I think it was probably pressure from his wife that prompted him a few years ago to make us promise that we wouldn't tell the girls about us. He would like to let them ask their own questions in their own time. However, I do recall overhearing Tina, my eldest granddaughter asking why granny Beth and granny Marj were sleeping in the same bedroom, and my son explained that as they had all come to stay, there wasn't very much room so some people had to share. I don't see the problem myself. What is he worried about? That the girls are going to think that he's gay because his mother's a lesbian? Before too long I'm just going to tell him that if he doesn't come clean with the girls, I will. I'd prefer to tell them anyway, in my own words, not apologetically. It won't make a bit of difference to the girls, I'm sure. We all get on famously.

Bert, 59, father to two adult sons and grandfather to one grandchild. *Surrey*.

I'm as open as I can be with my grandson. The unfortunate thing for him is not that his granddad is gay. That actually makes me a more understanding, accepting and emotionally aware granddad as I've worked through accepting who I am, and can be happy about accepting people for who they are, instead of wanting to change them. What I am sad about for my grandson is that he is now from a broken home, as my sons were. I left my marriage and the family home when my sons were under ten, and I was finally admitting to myself that the marriage was hell and that I might be gay. My sons are both heterosexual, and they were both married; now they are both divorced. So my grandson lives with his mother and sees his dad as much as possible. It doesn't matter what the parenting arrangement is – gay, lesbian, straight, biological parents or not, fostered or adopted – it is possible to have a committed, loving, bonded relationship between parent and child in any set-up. But for a single parent, I think it is inordinately difficult. The benefit for the child of being in a household of many loving people who provide role models of supportive, secure relationships is an incredibly rich upbringing. So, for my grandson, I will always be there, and I will be who I am: an honest, loving presence. His mother discourages him from seeing too much of me, not because I'm gay, but because she doesn't like him coming for rides on my motorbike. She's very worried about the safety aspect. I'm not going to be pushy about it, that would be counter-productive, but I am going to be there for him – that is how it is going to be – whoever wants to be encouraging or discouraging – I am his grandfather.

Notes

1. S. Golombok and F. Tasker (1995) Adults raised as children in lesbian families. *American Journal of Orthopsychiatry*, 65(2): 203–15.

2. See also 'Siobhan's' story in Chapter 8 and 'Glenda's' story in Chapter 9, for other examples of grandparent relationships.

FIFTEEN

The Shape of Things to Come?

The Albert Kennedy Trust

Historically, most lesbians and gay men became parents within an apparently heterosexual marriage, before coming out. In recent decades, however, increasing numbers of lesbians and gays are becoming parents *after* coming out.[1] This marked difference, particularly among lesbian parents, has led some to observe what they see as a lesbian baby boom.[2] The apparent gradual increase in acceptance of lesbians and gays when they are the natural parents (as shown in some of the cases featured in Chapter 9, where custody was awarded to same sex-couples in preference to the heterosexual families who brought the challenges) would have been almost unheard of only a few years ago. However, the problems facing lesbians and gays in other routes to parenthood are more persistent, especially when fostering and adoption is being considered. As we have seen in earlier chapters, the prejudices, although not backed up by any facts or research findings, perpetuate the myth that the sexuality of any children placed with lesbians and gays is more likely to develop in a homosexual direction (which is seen as an undesirable outcome), and for gender and sexual identity to become confused – false, but enduring, folklore about queer parents.[3-8] The work of the Albert Kennedy Trust (AKT) has shown very clearly that, if the sexuality of the children is already apparent, much of the reluctance to allow lesbians and gays to foster can be overcome. By assuming a pro-active stance, the Trust has pioneered the creation of positive and constructive environments in which to bring up lesbian and gay young people, in particular teenagers. It certainly is the shape of things to come for the building of a healthy, self-supporting and respected lesbian and gay community . . . 'looking after our own'. The rest of this chapter is devoted to AKT's pioneering work in bringing new definitions of parenting to the lesbian and gay community, *with* the support and encouragement of the relevant authorities.

The Albert Kennedy Trust (in the words of one of the trustees)
The Albert Kennedy Trust was set up following the death of the gay teenager Albert Kennedy in Manchester in 1989. He was in council care and had had a lot of problems with his own family and in his relationship with the social services. He'd been absconding from care, and going through phases of depression, rejection and rebellion. It was a very typical case of a young person who'd been abandoned by the system. It seemed to him nobody understood his sexuality, nobody wanted to deal with it, he was getting trapped into the familiar cycle of street-life problems. It culminated in a sad accident one day, where he and his boyfriend were trying to escape from a car-load of queerbashers, and went to the top of a car park in Manchester and, one way or another, he fell to his death. There's no evidence that he was pushed or that he jumped. That prompted the setting up of the Albert Kennedy Trust (AKT). The founder, a straight woman, was already fostering a gay teenager who was Albert Kennedy's boyfriend. So she knew how isolated Albert was, and how young people were being rejected because of their sexuality. Her foster son came home to her shortly after Albert had died in his arms. Out of this sad incident, the philosophy of the Trust grew; namely, that no lesbian or gay young person should feel so abandoned and so alone that that sort of problem could arise. She is the only person involved in the Trust who is straight. Although she is the founder, she feels she should never have got involved in the Trust in the first place. She is adamant that straights should not look after lesbian and gay young people. She kick-started AKT because there was no one else around to do it, and it was very difficult for out lesbians and gays to become foster parents. As soon as the Trust was up and running, with a sizeable group of lesbians and gays in charge, she stepped back, and is now the patron of AKT and continues to stress that it should only ever be lesbians and gays involved in organizing the Trust, being carers and running it.

The Trust has since developed its mission to help young lesbians and gays with *all* aspects of their lives, not just one issue, as soon as we can after problems occur. For example, as soon as they've been kicked out of their family homes, we'll take them on straight away. The Trust will find them accommodation with lesbian and gay families who act as positive role models; to let the young people see there are lesbians and gays who can live happy and fulfilled lives, even though things seem bad now. Also to tackle their problems generally, to do with self-esteem, how they make friends, more contact with the lesbian and gay community and to help them reconcile things with their parents. The Trust believes it is very important for the young people, ultimately, to get support and positive feedback from their parents. It is a fundamental factor in developing their inner peace. Their carers also help with finding a job or completing their education, and building the foundations for a balanced, self-sufficient life. It's much much more than just finding them a hostel or accommodation. The real problems facing lesbian and gay young people who are homeless, or having difficulties in care, are emotional problems around their own lives. For this reason the Trust provides a very high level of service. That means we have to have regular meetings with the young people and their social worker, with independent counsellors and other volunteers. Our carers get lots of help; independent meetings, people to support them, training and so on. So every placement involves a network of people supporting that placement.

The young people AKT help must self-identify as lesbian, gay or bisexual. They must be under twenty years old, and, in discussion with them, we have to feel that one of our placements is right for them. Below the age of sixteen, you can't take a young person into your house without the involvement of social services, because that would constitute 'harbouring a minor'. So, for teenagers who are sixteen or older, we approve our own carers, we make the placements and all the arrangements ourselves. For kids below the age of sixteen, the carers have to be approved by a local authority as registered foster carers, a social service department has to place the young person through AKT, and we then manage the placement. So there are two social services departments involved in the placement of a 'minor': one for the carers and one for the young person. AKT is the only organization involved in managing the placement day-to-day, so in practice there's not a big difference between the two types of placement, after the legal obligations have been met for the younger placements. Originally, it was mainly sixteen- or seventeen-year-olds whom AKT was finding place-ments for, but increasingly now there is a wider spread of ages. We're getting more and more demands from fifteen-year-olds especially. The youngest we have placed is a twelve-year-old. These are all self-identified lesbian or gay young people. Consequently, we are now short of registered foster carers to care for the under-sixteens.

A lot of lesbian and gay teenagers are quite able to cope on their own and don't need the intensive support that we can provide. We don't just turn people away and they don't have to fill in an application form; we work with them to identify what's best for them. So since AKT started, we have made over seventy placements, but have actually helped almost 500 teenagers who are living on their own. Sometimes we'll get a call from a teenager who says they don't actually want to live in a family, that they are able to look after themselves, have a job and so on. But they need support when they have a problem, or are feeling lonely. If they're getting hassle from their landlord or the council or social services about their benefits, they need someone more official to back them up. For teenagers who have left our care, we carry on supporting them if they need help in the future.

In practice, we get to meet our young people in a number of ways. Often, they've been kicked out of the family home and they call us up. Sometimes youth groups, lesbian and gay helplines and other independent organizations will refer the young people to us. But we also get young people placed with us through referring agencies like the social services, Centrepoint, London Connection. A lot of ex-AKT kids will also refer people they meet to us.

We don't put a blueprint on the kind or type of relationship we wish to see develop between the young person and the family they're living with. It can be very varied. We try to avoid making it too parental. We are not about finding kids for lesbian and gay parents. We are there to help the young people, that's all. The fact that there are people in the lesbian and gay community who have a need to care for somebody else is great. But that's not the need we're trying to fulfil. If we were to stress the parenting side of things, we would get people coming in who misunderstand what it's about. They see it almost as ownership of a young person, they want to show off their 'kid' to their friends and colleagues. That may not be right for that young person. After all, many AKT kids will have had bad experiences with their own families and what parents are about. The terms or images of father and mother may be very loaded and negative terminology for them, and they may need to get outside that concept completely. There is also an age issue. We may take in a seventeen-year-old, and a few of our carers are quite young, from about twenty-six years old and upwards. It would be very strange for a teenager to say 'dad' to someone only ten years older than them. A lot of young people may actively want a parental figurehead, which may make them overly reliant and desperate for someone to look after them. This can lead to them becoming attention-seeking, almost like a spoilt child, rather than a confident, independent adult. So we down-play the parenting side of it, and view it basically as providing a supportive environment. Originally the terminology AKT used was to call the carers 'big brothers' and 'big sisters'. I find that a very strange terminology, personally, and think quite a few AKT people in London do too. But different kids have different approaches; some view the carers as older brothers and sisters, some want a parental view and think of them as their mum or dad, and some view their carers as a friend, guardian or buddy they can go and talk to. We also stress to the carers that they shouldn't have a specific role in mind for their young person, for example, 'I expect him to be a good son to us.' It is important for us not to push any of these models onto the young person. We let that relationship develop on its own. When a young person comes forward, the AKT placement worker will decide who the most suitable available couple or carer is at that time. But AKT doesn't have a huge fund of carers, and sometimes they already have someone in mind as the first placement. You first get to meet your young person when the placement worker brings him or her to your home for a chat or a meal. The young person and the carers then have time to think about it and decide if they both want to proceed to the next stage. This involves the young person dropping round for the odd day or evening here and there, maybe staying over a weekend, so you can all gradually get to know each other better. The Trust likes this stage to go on as long as possible, at least a month or six weeks, because through experience, they know the longer this stage is, the more likely the placement is to work. The problem comes for young people in care who so often are desperate to get out, that as soon a carer expresses a willingness to accept them into their home, they can't wait to do it. Also, carers who've been waiting for a while may be tempted to rush into it. Only if both parties are completely happy will it go ahead. The Trust gives the carers as much information about the young person as is available to them, except for their HIV status, which is deemed irrelevant. It shouldn't make any difference to the carers' commitment, and it is up to the young person if they choose to disclose that information. But that's an area that hasn't yet happened with the Trust.

Placements are very expensive, at least £4000 each at present. The young person receives pocket money, the carers receive a small payment towards food and clothing. A lot of the young people placed with AKT are encouraged to continue with their education and the older teenagers will therefore not get benefits, and they have no one else to support them. AKT's money comes mainly from charitable trusts like CRISIS and Save the Children, plus Manchester City Council. Local authority money comes in as fees for AKT managing placements for young people. Donations from the lesbian and gay community are a small part of our income at the moment, but we are trying to increase that, to give us independence from some of the restrictions that apply to money from some sources.

There was a lot of controversy about AKT. Charity status was a long time coming because of the sensitivity of the issues the Trust deals with. Developing relationships with many different social services departments was a slow process too. The Trust had to try and convince them that if they have lesbian and gay young people in their care, then the best people to help them are lesbian and gay carers. We understand their problems, we understand what they're dealing with, we understand the root cause of what's creating their 'bad' behaviour. By 1996, a whole string of local authorities, of all political persuasions, had placed young people with AKT.

The Trust wants to become more of a community organization, proud to be offering leadership in this way, and to achieve wide knowledge and support in the lesbian and gay community. AKT now has a full-time placement worker who manages all the placements and our office is in Manchester. AKT's next goal is to have an office and a full-time placement worker in London. The homeless problem in London is huge, and many of those young people will be lesbian and gay. The goal for the next few years is to have offices and workers in Birmingham, Brighton, Edinburgh, Leeds and Liverpool.[9]

Caring for a child from the day he or she is born is a very different prospect to suddenly becoming responsible for a teenager, especially as many of the carers with the Albert Kennedy Trust will not have had their own children. A lot of the problems and dilemmas we heard of in Chapter twelve disappear when the teenager self-identifies as lesbian or gay, but that does not mean it is all plain sailing, as the following three case histories of AKT placements show.

Mark, 40, and Hassan, 31, have been carers to three Albert Kennedy Trust teenagers. *London*.

We have a natural caring instinct, and just because we're gay doesn't mean we don't have the same feelings everyone else does. We chose not to have our own children, so it seemed natural to care for other people's cast-offs and rejects that they can't handle. It wasn't a parental drive that made us want to do this. Also, they're teenagers, they're with you for a year or so and they're off; so 'Oh, I want a baby' is not an appropriate perspective or desire for becoming an AKT parent. We wanted to fix things that we thought were outrageous. You just can't help but be moved by some of these kids' stories. We almost screamed with anger at some of the things they've been through. It's just so outrageous that this is still going on, that we had to do something about it, and this is the most controlled way that we could get into doing it. At times you just want to bang your head against a brick wall, but you know that the only way to do something about it is by helping, even though you can only take a small number of kids, just one or two; that's what drove us to do it. Lots of people who get into fostering or caring of any sort may not have kids of their own and they look at the way that some other people treat children. It's a real privilege that those people have, and they abuse it incredibly. Why must they abuse kids because they don't fulfil their expectations of what their kids should be like? You do become very angry. We identify specifically with the issue of being lesbian or gay and the trauma that that entails for so many young people, the rejection for so many of them because they're not what their parents expect them to be. It's quite common for parents to be violent towards their children, and being lesbian or gay can be as good a reason as any. One teenager we heard of came out to his parents when he went home for Christmas, and he was then not allowed to drink from the same cups as the other children, and he wasn't allowed to use the toilet, he had to go out in the garden. This wasn't just an irrational belief that if he was gay he therefore must also be HIV-positive; they couldn't handle the whole issue of him being gay. He used to get beaten too, before and after coming out. We can't understand how so many parents can reject their children in the way they do.

We could have been fathers ourselves, there are many ways for gay men to achieve that. But we don't equate that with being AKT carers.

This isn't a replacement for a romantic notion of having our own kids. We want to help young people with their lives, and help them to set themselves up. We have recently gained approval as foster carers with our local authority. When we first applied they asked us if we wanted to adopt or foster. We had to think long and hard about that; did we want to adopt a one-year-old child? For us that seemed strangely possessive, almost a selfish act in many respects. It felt like we were looking for something to own by adopting a child. Some people seem to have kids as an accessory to their lives and we didn't want that. We wanted to help those young people already here who are having a hard time. Incidentally, we found that it would be easier for a gay man or lesbian to adopt than to foster. If you apply to foster as a gay couple, both of you have to be approved, and that's more difficult as a lesbian or gay couple. But what happens in practice for adoption is that one of you goes forward as the adoptive parent, even though everyone knows you're living with someone of the same sex. It's an easier process, but it's not what we wanted to do. We also wanted to make a point that we are a gay male couple, and we wanted to be accepted on the strength of what we would be as carers. Luckily we found a council who are supportive in that way. Once we've completed the training the council provides for all approved carers, the next question is whether the other social workers will make placements with us. There's a hell of a shortage of good carers at the moment and we think we can make good carers. Of course as registered carers for the local authority there is no guarantee that we will get lesbian or gay kids placed with us, and I'm sure we'll do just as good a job because we really care. Having had older placements from AKT has changed us. We are able to take a lot more stick. The reason we went for approval by our local authority was so that we could take younger lesbian or gay kids through AKT, who are very short of lesbian or gay people registered as foster carers. But in truth we care just as much about straight kids, as long as it doesn't hinder our ability to help lesbian and gay kids through AKT. After all, it is difficult for an under sixteen-year-old lesbian or gay teenager to find a placement with a lesbian or gay family, as there are so few of us registered. But we have a big house with plenty of space, so we could take more than one placement at a time, so we have no problem helping any young person in trouble. But also, if we went to the local authority and said we only want you to place self-identifying lesbian or gay kids with us, we wouldn't get anyone placed with us. Most local authorities, particularly within children's homes and among residential carers, have such a negative environment for young people to come out, that they very rarely do. In our experience, if you go and talk to social workers and say, 'How many lesbian or gay kids do you have in care?', very often they'll say, 'None'. But if you are more specific and say to them, 'How many male kids do you have who abscond from care, who are engaged in prostitution, who have had problems with gross indecency charges, who nobody seems to be able to talk to, nobody understands or knows who their friends are, who disappear off at weekends?', they'll say they've got hundreds. They will also admit that hardly ever are they able to get close enough to understand what their problems are. For these reasons, we know registered lesbian and gay foster carers who have gone to their local authorities and asked for only lesbian or gay teenagers to be placed with them and have had no placements made at all. It's because the systems and environment for kids to come out and be identified and supported isn't set up. The straight woman who founded the Albert Kennedy Trust maintains that straights cannot look after lesbian and gay kids. She's tried it. But she insists that lesbians and gays can look after straight kids. Her rationale is simple. The whole of society tells you to be straight and there are thousands upon thousands of images, role models, examples to draw on. Whatever your sexuality, you will have had a lifetime of information, examples and training in how to live, how to cope and what to aspire to in a heterosexual society. These are ample reasons for why lesbians and gays could do a good job looking after straight kids. There are virtually none of these provisions for lesbians and gays. You certainly aren't bombarded with imagery and information, let alone examples of successful and contented lesbian and gay pathways through life. Consequently, a straight kid growing up in a lesbian or gay household will have no problems around their self-identity, what it means to be straight, what it means to be male or female. But the other way round is a problem. People caring for lesbian or gay kids need to empathize about the situation, and need to understand what their situation is about. Most minorities need to be cared for by people from the same minority, but not the other way round. For the same reasons, black people can be excellent carers for white kids, but the other way round is more of a problem. If your racial background is so under-represented in the common consciousness, people outside of that community will have little or no contact with it. So, a teenager who has grown up in that culture or needs to be introduced into living in that community requires placement with carers from that minority. In our case, we wouldn't want two placements from AKT at the same time, although we would happily have two young people to care for at the same time. In our experience, the young people we've had so far from AKT have had a lot of problems, and it would be very difficult dealing with two conflicting sets of problems at the same time. Local authority placements of heterosexual young people are more likely to be younger, and won't have the rejection problems in the same way as the older lesbian or gay kids from AKT so often have, so that combination we feel would be manageable. The differences would bring a mutual support, rather than a competition between two older kids in such a similar situation.

When we first heard about the Albert Kennedy Trust we thought, 'Wow', we didn't even know this sort of thing could be, let alone that it already existed. But it's not the sort of thing you rush into. The idea grew over a few years, and when we were in a stable, long-term situation, job and house-wise, we applied. The application process, quite rightly, is very long and intensive, including interviews, assessment days, police checks and all sorts of things. In total it took over a year and a half for us to get approved as AKT carers. Now there are more people working for the Trust it takes about a year. It was good to have that amount of time, because it enabled us to think about it very deeply and seriously, to assess our reasons for doing it and to consider dropping out at any point. We can't help wishing that all people who go into parenthood or caring for kids would think and plan equally long and hard about it. Another good aspect is the way you advance to the next stage by writing in and requesting consideration. It allows you to progress at the rate appropriate to your situation, and ensures you are consciously making those decisions, not merely being swept along with the momentum of the application system. The time is very useful; when you have a partner, the most difficult thing is learning to live with that person and not being selfish. So bringing a third person into your life and home, particularly placements who can sometimes be disruptive, can have a major effect on your own relationship. But that's one of the reasons lesbians and gays make good carers; because it's not expected of us, you really do think about it before you do it, and you only do it if you're really committed to it. There's no reason why you should become a carer if you don't want to. You can go off and live a completely free life, being independent, no questions asked. We don't have these expected roles to fall into. Some people complain that the process takes so long, but we think it is a good thing.

We got nervous about telling people about our intentions, in case we didn't get accepted. We told a few close friends before we were accepted, and our families, but that was it. Most people don't think you can do it, it's not something they know about, not something lesbians and gays are perceived to do, so we expected negative reactions and kept quiet. Some people told us we were mad, but deep down most people shared our desire to help young people, once we talked to them at length. In fact, a lot of our friends can envisage a time, once they're financially and personally in a more settled position, when they would also want to become carers. We're not sure our experiences with some of the young people since have convinced them that that is a good idea. We had incredible problems with the first young man who came along. We actually took him on very quickly. AKT doesn't have a huge fund of carers, and in fact, when our final approval was being considered, they already had someone in mind as our first placement. The period between our first meeting and him moving in was only about two weeks, because he was pushing for it because he wanted to get out of care, and we put pressure on because we were keen to get started after an eighteen-month wait for final approval. Normally the Trust likes a longer approval period, and this rush may have caused a lot of our early problems. He wasn't a very difficult case as it turned out. He was very much an attention-seeking youngster who wanted us to be a replacement family. He was adopted at the age of two by a childless middle-class couple who couldn't handle the discovery later in life that he was gay. They had wanted him to be exactly what they had planned out for him, and he turned out to be very different. They eventually kicked him out because they couldn't handle him being gay and occasionally running away to see a boyfriend. Unless he was prepared to change and be straight, they weren't prepared to have him in their house. So he'd been rejected twice, by his natural parents, and now by his adoptive parents. He wanted us to be his parents, and he still calls us both dad, even though he's nearly nineteen now. He insists we are his replacement family. It may seem hard, but we are still gradually trying to convince him we are not and never can be a replacement for his family, but we are here to help and support him. He was disruptive in the sense that he sought attention the whole time, he demanded that our friends instantly became his friends, and not everyone wants an over-eager seventeen-year-old clasping them round the neck and kissing them profusely as a best friend the first time they meet. It was an over-familiarity that is very difficult to handle. He immediately regarded us as being his two fathers, and he would sit between us and cuddle up, which, with a seventeen-year-old, was quite a difficult thing for us to get used to. The thought of a seventeen-year-old boy cuddling up between two gay men is something that's going to send a lot of straight people into complete apoplexy, because they'll see it as some kind of sexual contact. But we'd had some training about the point where you need to show affection, but that young people, particularly these kind of young people, aren't necessarily good at understanding where the barriers between affection and sex are. I have to say that neither of us would be the slightest bit interested in him or any young person we were caring for. In retrospect I think we were over-anxious to please, we sympathized immensely with his background, he'd had a really tough time, and we were spoiling him initially. Had we had a longer time to get to know him we might well have developed a better strategy than allowing ourselves to be manipulated on many issues. We felt uncomfortable with the cuddling on the sofa incident, so we explained to him that affection was something we were happy to give him, a comforting kind of affection. But the kind of affection we felt he might be working towards was the sort Hassan and I show to each other, not the sort to share with him; in other words, clarifying the different levels of affection that mean different things, and when and where these were appropriate. In fact I don't think he meant anything sexual by his behaviour, it was just that through absconding from the children's home and having sex with people, it was the only kind of comfort he had. He needed to learn that you could get comfort and affection from people without actually having some kind of sexual contact as well. He had problems learning what was appropriate. When we had our first meeting with the social services department that was approving us, two weeks after he was placed with us, the woman who visited us was very upset when she saw him walking round the house in just his underpants. She thought that was completely inappropriate behaviour for him;

perhaps she was being a bit picky, but he certainly did have problems knowing what was appropriate. It improved slowly over the time he was with us, and now he is much more aware of what is socially acceptable. He is always eager to please, to gain acceptance. He was also very loud, and ran up huge phone bills – you know, all the usual teenage things as well. But in fact, he was quite mild in comparison to some of the placements other AKT carers have had. At the time it seemed very difficult, especially as we never really knew if he was telling us the truth. He was very promiscuous, which in itself we tried not to be judgmental about, but in his case it was because he didn't value himself. We sat him down one day and said, 'Wouldn't it be nice if you actually knew somebody for a while before having sex with them? That they actually valued you as a person, rather than just an object to have sex with.' He met a very nice young man shortly after that and they went out for two weeks, and he made a point of telling us that they hadn't had sex yet. He got a phone call from this guy asking him if he wanted to come over and stay the night. He asked us and we said, 'Well yes, it's not a problem. As long as you know what you're doing and you think it's OK.'

The guy dumped him immediately after they'd been to bed. I think that taught him some kind of lesson that it is what people want from him. It's a slow process, but he is changing and has learned from that, that there is more than just sex. We still get problems even though he's moved into his own flat now. He'll phone us in the middle of the night with a big drama, or we'll have boyfriends or families of boyfriends coming to the house or shouting through the letterbox. He wanted to stay on forever, but when he turned eighteen we said it would be better if he started looking for his own place and became independent. It's not in his interests for us to stop him becoming independent. He was with us for about a year, and didn't want to leave at the end. He had a job, and eventually found a place, and reflecting on it now, he sees the wisdom of our encouraging him to become independent. We felt bad about it, as if we were failing him in some way, because it felt like we were rejecting him as well. I think we explained it well enough though, to show him we would always be here for him, but that he must start to stand on his own two feet. I can't deny we felt slightly relieved as well. Just like when you have a relative to stay for a long time, however much you love them, when they first go you feel how nice it is finally to be on your own for a while. When you're eighteen you're an adult and you have to think about planning for the rest of your life instead of intending to rely on other people to support you. Part of the problem we've found so often with young people who've been in care is that they are reliant on other people, they don't seem to have the ability to support themselves. They feel the world owes them a living almost, and they can get whatever they want just by asking or by protesting they've had a really bad life so far so you should give them what they want. But it's not helping them, not to let them go. He's been back here for the last two Christmases and we go round to his new flat for dinner occasionally, so we do keep in touch pretty well. We tried to encourage him to re-establish contact with his parents, but they didn't want to know, and even his grandmother, who wanted to keep in touch, was under instructions not to have any involvement. He wanted to go to Germany on an exchange visit with a friend, but as a seventeen-year-old his parents needed to sign his passport form. They refused to sign it saying, 'He hasn't done anything for us, why should we do anything for him?'

I'm proud of lots of small things we've achieved. You can never fix someone in a year or two after they've been through sixteen years of trouble. You end up fixing small things that you realize later were incredibly significant. Things like looking after themselves, personal hygiene, how often they have a good meal, how regularly they have the inner peace to stay in their own home and not sleep somewhere else. Those things we're definitely proud of. If I think of the spoilt brat who came to us as our first placement and see the young man he has become, with his own flat, a long-term relationship, the ability to hold down jobs reasonably well, it's incredibly gratifying.

Simon, 45, and Denis, 35, carers to Jack, 17. *London*.

Jack's social worker decided that as he used to go to the West End a lot, and always had more money than he should have, he was clearly more than he seemed to be. He'd never said he was gay, but she felt that maybe the Albert Kennedy Trust was the place for him, that he maybe gay. She gave him information on the Trust, and eventually he said it might be something he would be interested in. On the way to see us for the first time he apparently said to his social worker, 'I don't want to live with a couple of poofs', but when he met us it was very obvious to us that he was gay, but wouldn't admit it to himself. His family were very resistant to him being placed with us, but as he was officially 'at risk', social services could decide where he was going to stay. He came to stay with us for the weekend and I gave him a lift back to his grandmother's, where he was staying at the time. I met her and we got on very well. When it came to the formal placement meeting at the social services department his mother changed her mind and decided to come. When she met us she realized we weren't such bad people after all and was totally converted. In fact one of our greatest successes with him is that his sexuality is now not a problem for him or his family. There are many other problems still, but him being gay is no longer one of them. His dabbling with prostitution has stopped too. He was our second placement and he had the largest room in the house; the top-floor room we'd had specially done out, with his own TV, and he liked it very much. We wanted him to have somewhere he could get away from us if he wanted to. Unfortunately, being quite an introverted young man, after he moved in he wouldn't come out of his room for long periods at a time, and it wasn't until we took his television out that we encouraged him to come down and speak to us. He'd been in a children's home and had missed school for a number of years. One thing that became very obvious to us very quickly was that he was deaf in one ear. Nobody else had noticed this, which is surprising, because he'd been in local authority care for years and his mother had also never spotted it. Whenever he talked, he would turn his head to one side, and he talked slightly out of the side of his mouth, on the side that he could hear. It just shows how much attention he received in his first seventeen years of life. Apart from his other problems, since he probably couldn't hear properly at school it's no wonder he didn't do well. It all started off very well with him, he was quiet and nervous, but very keen to be part of our family. Then for no apparent reason, about a month after he moved in with us, he disappeared. This is apparently quite common, but at the time we took it as a real failure on our part. Young people who've been living on the streets or in a situation where they don't have to be self-disciplined can find it difficult to conform to a more organized, responsible environment. So he just had to get away for a while and live in more familiar surroundings to him, to be able to readjust, realize how bad his former situation was, before he could came back again. We were tearing our hair out, informing the police, telling the social services; we couldn't understand why the social workers weren't that bothered about it and took it as quite natural behaviour. God, have we grown up and seen the real world since caring for these kids! Anyway, after about a week of hearing absolutely nothing, he phoned us up and said he was coming back. He arrived wearing completely different clothes and we never again saw the clothes he'd been wearing when he left. We sat him down and wrung our hands and said, 'Why didn't you phone us and tell us where you were and that you were OK?' He didn't seem to have any explanation for running off, but he seemed pleased to be back with us. His disappearing act happened a few more times, and we eventually came to terms with it. He also became more and more disruptive in many ways. We hadn't been told how much of a problem he had with people. The first time the social worker from AKT came to see him, she arrived for dinner with a student social worker assistant. Jack wouldn't come into the room, he caused a bit of a scene and ran to his room. The social worker went upstairs and coaxed him down, and he ended up getting on very well with the social worker assistant. He was due to start a college course that would give him a cross-section of experience on various jobs. The course tutor had explained the format of the course and he seemed keen to do it, even up until the night before, but on the first morning of the course he just wouldn't go. So Denis took him along to the college, but Jack just sat outside and wouldn't go in. Then he disappeared again, because he felt if he came back we'd have a go at him. We felt perhaps we couldn't help him and said it might be better if people who could handle him became his carers. So for about a month he left us, but kept in touch. We slowly realized we'd jumped the gun a bit and made a mistake; we'd pushed him too hard. We didn't realize just how much difficulty he had just handling contact with people. So he came back to live with us again. He finally told us he didn't go into college that day because he'd have had to go into a room full of strangers, and he couldn't handle that. So we adopted a different approach, trying to encourage him rather than push him. This was different from the advice from his social worker who told us we should set rules and make him do things. What worked with him in the end was to stand back and let him do things at his own pace. So I took him in to work at my own business. It enabled him to come in with me, to meet just a small group of people who know I'm gay and have no problem with me or him being gay. He also had to talk to customers occasionally. Gradually, all this built up his confidence with people, to the point where recently he was able to walk into a room of fifteen new volunteers for the Trust and hold a conversation with a few of them without any problem. So we feel we've certainly helped him on that side.

Jack had felt rejected all his life, by his parents, the children's home, by his clients when he was a rent boy, and he couldn't believe that we wouldn't reject him, so he kept pushing us to see how far he could go. We accepted quite a lot from him; he wrecked our house, he stole a car (not ours) while he was drunk, crashed it and was arrested, he became violent towards a few people, including a boyfriend who took out assault charges against him, but dropped them when they got back together. There was a series of gradually worsening events, but we accepted them all and told him we understood, that he wasn't going to push us into rejecting him, that we did like him, and he is a nice kid. When he's being good he's one of the most pleasant people I've met: very good company, very chatty now. But his whole sense is of not being wanted when he feels cornered or insecure. He thought all we were doing for him was false; he told people we were getting paid £1000 a week to keep him. He had to believe there was some other reason for us doing it other than we liked him and wanted to help him. In fact, when he came back to us after the month's break, we weren't receiving any funding, and this seemed to impress him more than anything. He couldn't figure out what we were doing it for. He knew it wasn't money now. Ultimately, the placement had to end because he became violent to Denis and that we couldn't accept. We have seen him quite a lot since, we phone each other regularly and he is growing up quite a lot. He actually said to us recently that he appreciated what we've done for him. He'd never said that before, and it's not what you expect young people to say. So it certainly seems to have done some good for him. Ultimately, you're never sure how well it is working. You always feel you've failed because they very rarely achieve the kind of independence and status in life you'd like them to. But when his social worker says to us, 'Jack's getting on really well', and it doesn't seem that good to us, she'll say, 'Well, he's combing his hair and he's washing more frequently, he feels better about himself.' Achievement is relative, we've realized.

I think it's quite difficult to know what being AKT parents or carers has done for us as a couple. We've been through a heck of a lot of problems, a lot of stress, but ultimately it's another experience you have that brings you closer together, more intimately bonded. It's helped us evaluate what our real priorities are in life, what we really want to do. It puts your own problems into perspective when you see what these young people have had to face in their lives. It helps you see your whole life in a wider context, it makes you grateful for what you've got. Co-parenting has cemented our relationship, but there wasn't really any distance between us. That would have been the wrong reason to become carers, in the hope that it would bring us closer together or solve some problems we had with commitment to each other. It is so often the reason you hear from straight couples, that they hoped having kids would save the marriage. In fact, for a couple who aren't so close, parenting, I think, will move them further apart. Being carers has enabled us to handle crises a little bit better, so when there's a real emergency I think we could handle that more effectively. The way we worked together has been very satisfying; on our own it would have been very difficult. I'm most proud that we were able to take an awful lot and accept it as the product of the life Jack's had; rather than getting self-righteous and saying, 'I'm not having that', we were able to accommodate it. It cost us a lot in terms of damage to the house, but that doesn't matter. We judge ourselves very harshly, but I can see we transformed Jack totally as a person, from someone who was really embarrassed about being gay. He used to say he hated queers, that he hated being gay, he thought that sex was never pleasurable, it was always an experience used for money or because someone was trying to get something out of you. To be transformed from that into somebody who's confident, outgoing, able to give his boyfriend a peck on the cheek in public is totally astonishing. He's also started mincing a lot more; I don't know why that is. He is now strangely intolerant of people who aren't out. There is almost a sense of relief when you see these changes, because so often you can't be sure you're doing any good. Also, there's a real sense of pride too. It's easy to believe that life is all about making a success of things and making money, but for us now, being able to help people is just as important.

Annie, 38, and Martina, 43, carers for Stephen, 19. *Manchester*.

It's a bit unusual really for us to have a male placement at the moment, especially as there are fewer lesbian registered carers in AKT than there are gay men. However, there were no male carers available when Stephen needed an emergency placement, so he came to us. We were lucky to have a gay male friend staying with us when Stephen arrived, so he was able to sort out a few problems that we would have found more difficult. Stephen doesn't have the same problems as many AKT kids. His mother is very antagonistic about his sexuality and is very unhappy about him 'playing the field' as she sees it, ever since he split up with a boyfriend that she did approve of. He was coming up to taking his A-levels and the pressure from his mother was becoming too much and stopping him concentrating on his exams. So he contacted AKT, and he was happy to come to us as a placement, especially as we live close to his college. We're not able to be much of a gay male role model to him as two lesbians, which causes some problems, but we do have a lot of gay male friends that he's in contact with and he does have his own network of young gay men as well, so he's not lacking role models. In fact he calls me mother and Martina father, which she doesn't mind. He's only with us until he takes up his guaranteed place at university in the autumn, so to some extent we're mainly providing accommodation. He's nineteen, so he's much more mature than other placements we've had, but there have been moments when he's needed our advice. We're also learning from him. We understand that gay men face prejudices and we're often tempted to think it's a man's world so they can't be that badly off, but it's been a learning process for us to see the day-to-day examples that we perhaps weren't aware of. If we get another male placement we'll be better equipped to deal with it. In fact, we're building up this little family. Last Christmas we had Ruth and Paula, our first two placements, here. Next Christmas it'll be Ruth, Paula and Stephen; you don't lose them when they leave you, hopefully they're still friends, and if they have any problems in life that they can't go to their parents about, then we'll be the next step. It certainly happened with Ruth, our first placement, who is in regular contact and calls to discuss problems. Paula less so, because she doesn't tend to talk about her problems, but I'm sure she'd come to us if there was something really troubling her. It's a nice feeling that we have a network of young people who are also starting to help each other.

Notes

1. C. J. Patterson (1994) *Current Directions in Psychological Science*, 3(2): 62–4.

2. *Ibid.*

3. M. King and P. Pattison (1991) Homosexuality and parenthood. *British Medical Journal*, 303: 295–7.

4. R. Langevin (1983) *Sexual Strands. Understanding and Treating Sexual Anomalies in Men*. London: Lawrence Erlbaum.
5. J. R. Conte (1991) The nature of sexual offences against children. In C. R. Hollen and K. Howells (eds), *Clinical Approaches to Sex Offenders and Their Victims*. Chichester: John Wiley, pp.11–34.
6. G. Abel, J. Becker, J. Cunningham-Rather, M. Mittleman and J. L. Rouleau (1988) Multiple paraphilic diagnoses among sex offenders. *Bulletin of American Academy of Psychiatry Law*, 16: 153–68.

7. D. Finkelhor and D. Russell (1984) Women as perpetrators: review of the evidence. In D. Finkelhor (ed.), *Child Sexual Abuse: New Theory and Research*. New York: Free Press, pp. 171–87.
8. See fuller discussion in Chapter 9 on homosexuals being no greater a risk to children than heterosexuals.
9. As of summer 1996, funding and staff for an office in London are yet to be found. However, the London and other regional offices still intend expansions for the Albert Kennedy Trust.

SIXTEEN

Advice

With the benefit of hindsight, some lesbian and gay parents would do things differently, others wouldn't change a thing, but it is certainly worth taking note of their advice to prospective lesbian and gay parents.

Glenda, 31, who co-parents with Sally, 40, their daughter Nerys, 4. *Southampton.*

Go for it; the pain's worth it. It's sheer agony, but it's definitely worth it. Sally and I are at home most of the time, and our lives focus around our daughter. We try to make sure she doesn't get too dependent on us. So, one day a fortnight she's off with friends and the other week we have her friends over here. Try to be a bit more careful than we were with the donor. Have your donor screened; we didn't know how to go about it then, so we just took his word that he was healthy. It was a bloody dangerous thing to do, but at the time he was our only choice. Go to a donor insemination clinic if you can afford it or draw up your own list of medical questions and go with him to get the results.[1] It's your life and the baby's life you're playing with.

Daniel, 32, separated from his wife Bridget, 31, and two daughters Ruth, 6, and Mary, 4. *Aberdeen.*

My advice to prospective lesbian and gay parents is DON'T. Well, perhaps that's a bit strong, but now I know the complexity of parenting and what's involved I find the responsibility of parenthood onerous. A lot of us enter into it without an understanding of the massive task it is and that it affects every area of our lives. I also think lesbians and gays often have kids to achieve acceptance or 'normality'. I see an equal desperation in childless heterosexual couples, who are also often trying to compensate for something through their quest for children. Ask yourself, why do I really want kids?

Gareth, 37, donor father to three daughters – Sasha, 3, Ella, 2, and Alicia, 1 – by different mothers. *Surrey.*

Having children has made me calm down in my life and not keep looking around for something that was missing. The fulfilment that having children has given me has made me more able to conduct a stable relationship. I feel as if I'm not searching for something desperately any more. I'm much calmer about the life to come and how my life will unfold. The future for lesbian and gay parents lies in us becoming much more visible and far more of these arrangements going ahead. So many kids are brought into this world by accident and are unloved. All three of my daughters are wanted, loved and secure, and you can't give people a better start in life than that. The sexuality of the parent is immaterial. It is the relationship with the child that is important, and public attitudes to lesbian and gay parents are changing; we're becoming more acceptable.

I think all parents-to-be should discuss things very carefully with other parents-to-be and their partners. I met one or two other potential mothers besides the ones I proceeded with. There was one out lesbian who wanted her child to be brought up quite strictly Catholic, which I thought was loading guilt onto a child, so I didn't proceed with that invitation. Writing a letter setting out your proposals for access, and other terms on which you are happy to proceed, is also a good idea. It clarifies your requests and enables both sides to come to an adult and clear agreement for the parameters of bringing up the child. It isn't necessarily legally binding but it is very useful.,

Terry, 36, teacher and donor father. *London.*

You'll never think of everything. For example, it was decided my son would call me daddy, but with my daughter, her mother uses my first name to refer to me. It was one thing we never settled when we were discussing having a child . . . what I would be called. It's worth deciding in advance. If you can be reasonably sure that a sensible adult agreement can be met with your co-parents, on any subject, many difficulties can be avoided. If you can't agree on things in advance, will you be able to agree when the child has arrived and things really get hectic?

Simon, 38, and his lover Giles, 43, with Nita, 37, and Cheryl, 39, are co-parents to James, 8, and Edward, 6. *Kent*.

I think I'm very ill-placed to give advice, because we've run across so few problems that I haven't had the experience on which to educate myself. But I would say that one must be prepared to have a certain generosity of spirit and understanding towards the other parents, and to recognize that their emotions and feelings towards the child will be very strong, and that the child will benefit from an awareness that the bonds of affection between the various parents are very strong. So that if you are going to enter into a co-parenting relationship it does help to be very fond of the other parent. I don't know what it would be like to go into this cold through an advertisement. I'm not saying that's wrong, but I think that even in that situation if it's going to be co-parenting, and not just a donation, I think that one needs to give the child the awareness that the parents do at least like each other and get on well. I think that in the absence of any formal arrangement or agreement, which we did not make to start with, the genuine affection between the four of us before we ever thought of becoming parents has been the one thing that has made this a successful enterprise. It's been wonderful for all of us really.

I also think one has to be in some ways protective of the child's exposure to the world and the terms in which you've brought it into the world, as it were. These children are usually not conceived as a social experiment, but in some cases that is what they are going to be. You've got to protect them as far as possible from the need to be crusaders. You can't expect the child to crusade on the part of the right of gay people to have children. That's not what they are going to see their lives as being all about. And you've got to respect their integrity; of the child and the experience of the child. So I think that to some extent a certain degree of discretion may be necessary. After all, it's no different really from the fact that many families have secrets that they keep from the outside world, and that's not unreasonable. On the other hand, one has got to recognize that the sort of teenage problems that you would come across in all families would be possibly a little worse, because of the difficulties that children have to deal with.[5] I suppose I believe this because, when it comes down to it, their parents are still, in some senses, outlaws. I don't know, I suppose that in a white society black children also have a problem. But at least they are the same colour as their parents, so they are in the same community. Whereas the difference between gays and their children is that the children are very likely to be heterosexual, and not part of their parents' community. And whereas we can say, well, we weren't part of our parents' community either, our parents were not the outlaws, as it were. These are difficulties that every gay parent has to think about and be prepared to address. I don't say that it should be something that should put them off. I think probably that the more gay parents there are, the easier it will be. And one day gay parenting will burst upon the world. I suspect that in about ten years time when these children become teenagers and young adults, this sort of baby boom will become more visible.

Kirk, 37, whose partner Keith, 43, is the natural father to Kelly, 15, and Stuart, 18. *Leeds*.

It can be done and there's no real problem. But you've got to be very child-centred. We've given a lot of time to the kids, probably too much. They're very independent now, although Stuart is the quieter one and will be at home for quite a while yet, which is fine. It's also really important to be upfront and open about who you are. If you are ashamed or censoring about your situation it will breed a climate of shame, lack of self-respect and inhibition. Not a healthy way to be, I don't think. Living with integrity gives power. It also makes life easier and of a higher quality. For example, we are completely open with the schools and our doctor and dentist. If you are proud of yourselves and your family, you must claim your right to the same treatment and service as everyone else. I have found co-parenting an incredible learning process and to have the unconditional love of two young people is just brilliant. Now the kids are older, Keith and I can start to re-establish our links with the gay scene and community, although our relationship has changed so much with having kids, and there have been great strains and problems to resolve. But now we operate on so many different levels, the scene might seem a bit shallow – who knows? It's so gratifying to think of the smelly waifs we collected from their mother all those years ago and to see the balanced, happy young adults they are now. I wouldn't have missed being a parent for anything.

Graham, 47, father to Yvonne, 27. *London and Yorkshire.*

I always regret not having had more contact. It was a geographical thing really. I think that if you are going to have children, then it is a commitment. Everyone needs a lot of reassurance from another adult, and it's up to mature adults to provide that. I think that I was too young, not necessarily naive; it's only in retrospect that you realize things could have been done better. But hindsight's an easy thing. I think that the main thing is to keep in contact, be honest, be open. But I don't think that you should volunteer things necessarily, unless there was some kind of problem; I don't think that you should necessarily go round parading your sexuality.

Maggie, 36, and Shelley, 40, mothers to twins, 4. *London.*

If you're going to get pregnant, don't rely on anybody. Don't rely on anybody ever doing anything for you, and then if they do it's a real plus, a real bonus and it makes life wonderful. Don't have twins, if you can possibly avoid it, unless you have got a lot of mates. Take out insurance, . . . against having twins. Because if you don't take out insurance against having twins, you won't have very much money because you will have to buy two of everything and the DSS doesn't give you any of the money for that. And child benefit is worked on the logic that you have an older child and a younger child and so you don't get two lots of child benefit you only get one at the higher rate and one at the lower rate . . . The assumption is that with child benefit you get more money for the first child, because that's the first time you buy everything, and if you are going to have more children you keep everything, so therefore you get a lower rate of Child Benefit for subsequent children. But with twins you don't get two higher rates, even though you have to buy two of everything. Which just means that you can't afford to buy the two of everything you need. So you just have to beg, borrow, steal, whatever. And the government doesn't want to increase benefits.

Also, make sure you're in pension schemes, often private pension schemes, where you can assign the rights to your same-sex partner. We can't with our work pension schemes.

Gwen, 59, grandmother to Max, 1, and mother to Wendy, 30.
Liverpool.

Be out and be proud; make sure your kids are proud of you through living with integrity and honesty. Kids rarely have a problem with simple, honest, direct facts; it's the deceit and the secrecy that build shame and inhibition. If you have self-respect, then others respect you too. If you don't respect yourself enough to be yourself, how can you expect others to respect you? That's the greatest gift to any family, straight, gay or lesbian: living with integrity.

Jim, 38, single father to Hayley, 8, born to a surrogate mother. *Isle of Wight.*

On the practical side, you have to consider the impact that a child has on your lifestyle. But if it's in your heart, you will do it. I think you should follow your heart.

I don't think that the same-sex question should make any difference. If you want a child, you will get one. The key point for the child growing up is be totally honest. Don't hide the truth. If you lie to the child, then the people who say 'same sex couples can't have children' would be proved right; because you would screw the child up. You would do so much damage. You have to be honest. Kids don't have a problem with reality. They don't question. They give love and they take love and that's all there is to it. It doesn't matter about what your gender or sexuality is. That's the most important thing that I've learned; be honest. It's the problem that Jack and I stepped into; we'd told all these lies to cover up the surrogacy arrangement and we trapped ourselves. We were locked into this thing that we couldn't get out of. Only Jack leaving enabled all those lies to fall away. We told so many lies, for seven years . . . and you can never remember what you'd said, it all gets mixed up. Since living openly, I've been liberated, and life is so much easier for me and for my daughter.

Pam, 40, now separated from Rhona, 25, and their son, Nicky, 6. *Bristol.*

Be very wary of taking on other people's children and getting involved. I wouldn't say don't do it, but a conscious agreement about what will happen, the access arrangements and the financial commitments, saves a lot of heartache and insecurity if the worst does happen. I should have spotted the warning signs: reluctance to make any firm arrangements; Nicky's grandmother had a residence order as she'd been looking after Nicky before Rhona and I got together and she was blowing hot and cold about my involvement all along; the fact she had a residence order for Nicky made it very unlikely I would have got one. I am now very wary about ever again becoming a co-parent if I am not the natural mother. I'm not ruling it out, but I'd want firm, clear, adult agreements and decisions in advance.

John, now divorced, father to Gary, 11, and Emma, 10. *Hull.*

Whether they're gay or straight or whatever, my initial advice would be the same: think long and hard about it. You can say that to people and they never listen. Because I never did. People said to me, 'Don't have them unless you really want them.' You think 'Oh, it can't be that bad.' And then you get them and you realize how bad it can be. If you are going to live a completely gay lifestyle, you can more or less live your life completely the way you want to, you can go here, there and everywhere. If there is a child involved, then no; you can't bring up a child in that environment. A child needs stability and I don't think that a gay lifestyle is compatible with children. There are too many opportunities to go off and do other things. I think that if you are gay and that's the lifestyle that you want, then why do you want a child to drag you back? You know, you can't put it in kennels; have a dog instead.

But if you could have a one-to-one relationship and you knew you were going to be together for a long time, then I still don't think it would be a good idea, because a child, I think, needs to have input from the female and the male parent.[3] As a foursome, two lesbian and gay couples might solve that problem. I can't see any reason why that shouldn't happen or work. And of course having kids changes people.

When the kids are young particularly, you're always putting the kids first. Having kids puts a strain on all relationships, kids don't cement relationships. My other worry about a gay or lesbian couple having kids is that one of the couple is not going to be as committed to the child, because it's not theirs; it can't be. For a heterosexual couple having kids, the child is both of theirs. Blood is thicker than water is something I do believe. I know that knocks out step-parents and adoptive parents, but I believe there is a bond between the child and the natural parents, and it's no coincidence that so many adopted kids have a strong desire to find who their real parents are. That's not to say step-parents can't do a good job, but there isn't the same bond. My kids have a step-father now, and he also has two of his own kids and I often wonder, like in *Sophie's Choice*,[4] if he had a choice to save two of the kids, I bet you anything he'd save his own, not mine, because there is that sort of bond there.

Bert, 59, father to two adult sons and grandfather to one grandchild. *Surrey*.

It doesn't matter to me what combination of parents bring up a child – biological parents, adoptive parents, same-sex couples, extended families. It is always claimed that there is a special, deep, unique bond between the biological parents and their child; that no one else could be that devoted or unconditionally loving to the child. I think that is total crap. It is possible to form bonds with people you are not biologically related to that are every bit as strong as 'blood ties'. I have sort of adopted a younger gay couple as kind of my surrogate sons. They are now in their late twenties, but I have been their supportive, fatherly gay figure for many years and the bond between us is stronger than the one between me and my two sons. I am overwhelmed by the love, kindness and consideration my gay family shows to me. It far outstrips any overt signs of love and affection from my own sons.

To lesbian and gay prospective parents I would say, examine your motives for wanting children. Why do you need kids? For lesbian and gay parents it is more likely to be a creative urge than a status symbol. Single mums are vilified for being scroungers and irresponsible, and lesbian and gay parents certainly don't get widespread adulation. So you've got to have the strength to do it. The other thing I've discovered is that the most unexpected people will be supportive; the old lady next door, the colleague at work who you know votes Tory, your macho brother. Once they see what a wonderful family unit you have brought kids into, many people will be encouraging. You need to be sure you have a secure practical, financial and personal set-up and a supportive circle of friends and/or family.

In the heterosexual world you are taught that your kids and you have a unique bond, and that you can only love your own biological family as unconditionally. It is not true. I'm not a religious person but a story from the Bible springs to mind. When Jesus was about twelve, he was separated from his parents. When strangers asked him where his mother and father were he said, 'Who is my mother? Who is my father?' That means a lot to me. Who is my son? It is anybody; there's a whole world out there and one shouldn't be bound by meaningless rules. There does not have to be a biological or genetic relationship before there can be strength, love and unequivocal commitment to another human being. Potentially, anyone can be family.

Notes

1. See 'Summary of criteria for acceptance as a sperm donor (used by many UK donor insemination clinics)', in Appendix.
2. S. Golombok and F. Tasker (1995) Adults raised as children in lesbian families. *American Journal of Orthopsychiatry*, 65(2): 203–15.
3. For further discussion on research findings that show same-sex couples bringing up children do not cause gender or sexuality confusion, see Chapter 9.
4. *Sophie's Choice*, film starring Meryl Streep as a Polish woman who, during World War II, must choose which of her children to give up to guards in a concentration camp.
5. The pioneering work of Professors Golombok and Tasker of the City University, London (see note 2) has found that adults raised in lesbian families were no more likely to remember general teasing or bullying by their peers than were adults raised in heterosexual single-parent families. In addition, those that did experience hostility as children or as teenagers showed no differences between the lesbian or heterosexual families, in the seriousness with which they viewed or recalled the experiences. Even more encouraging is their finding that in adulthood men and women raised by lesbian mothers were no more likely than their peers from heterosexual single-parent homes to experience anxiety or depression, or to have sought professional help for mental health problems.

Summary of Criteria for Acceptance as a Sperm Donor

(used by many UK donor insemination clinics)

The following medical conditions are the main criteria used by many UK donor insemination clinics to decide whether or not to take on a potential sperm donor. The donor is asked to declare if he, his mother or father, any brothers or sisters, grandparents or other relatives have or have had any of the following conditions or medical problems. The criteria marked with an asterisk (*) would be or may be the subject of a blood test.

HIV*
AIDS (or other immune
   deficiency) *
Haemophilia
Sickle cell anaemia
Leukaemia
Hepatitis (A,B,C) *
Anaemia*
Other blood disorders

High blood pressure
High cholesterol
Heart attack
Palpitations
Stroke
Thrombosis
Hardening of arteries
Other heart disease
Rheumatic fever

Lung cancer
Colon cancer
Intestinal/stomach cancer
Liver cancer
Cervix/uterus/ovary cancer
Thyroid cancer
Testicular cancer
Skin cancer
Breast cancer
Prostate cancer
Other cancer not covered above

Tuberculosis
Asthma
Pneumonia
Emphysema
Cystic fibrosis
Other lung diseases

Ulcers
Liver disease
Kidney/gall stones
Crohn's disease
Colitis

Hormonal disorders
Adrenal disorders
Thyroid disease
Diabetes mellitus
Kidney disease
Urinary tract disease
Endometritis
Ovarian cysts

Migraines
Mental illness (needing medical
treatment)

Schizophrenia
Depressive disorders
Alzheimer's disease
Epilepsy

Cerebral palsy
Multiple sclerosis
Huntington's chorea
Spinal cord/spine disorders
Other neurological diseases

Alcoholism
Drug abuse/addiction
Do you smoke?
Muscular dystrophy
Arthritis
Osteoporosis
Other muscle diseases
Deafness
Blindness
Cataracts (before age 50)
Any other sight, smell or hearing
disorder

Eczema
Skin/pigment disorders

Any other condition/disease not
covered above

Selected Reading

Baptiste, D.A. *The Gay and Lesbian Stepparent Family*. New York: Praeger Publishing, 1987.

Barret, R.L. and Robinson, B.E. *Gay Fathers*, Lexington, MA: Lexington Books, 1990.

Bosche, S. *Jenny Lives with Eric and Martin*. London: Gay Men's Press, 1981.

Bozett, F.W. (ed.) *Gay and Lesbian Parents*. New York: Praeger, 1987.

Bozett, F.W. and Sussman, M.B. (eds) *Homosexuality and Family Relations*. New York: Harrington Park Press, 1990.

Corley, R. *The Final Closet: The Gay Parents' Guide for Coming out to Their Children*. Miami: Editech Press, 1990.

Gochros, J.S. *When Husbands Come out of the Closet*. New York: Harrington Park Press, 1989.

Kurdek, L.A. (ed.) *Social Services for Gay and Lesbian Couples*. Binghamton, NY: The Haworth Press, 1994.

Maddox, B. *Married and Gay*. New York: Harcourt Brace Jovanovich, 1982.

McCandlish, B.M. *Against All Odds: Lesbian Mother Family Dynamics*. New York: Praeger Publishing, 1987.

Muller, A. *Parents Matter: Parents' Relationships with Lesbian Daughters and Gay Sons*. Tallahassee, FL: Naiad Press, 1987.

Newman, L. *Heather Has Two Mommies*. Boston: Alyson, 1989.

Parrot, A. and Ellis, M.J. *Homosexuals Should Be Allowed to Marry and Adopt or Rear Children*. Beverly Hills, CA: Sage Publishing, 1985.

Pennington, S.B. *Children of Lesbian Mothers*. New York: Praeger Publishing, 1987.

Pies, C. *Considering Parenthood: A Workbook for Lesbians*. San Francisco: Spinsters/Aunt Lute, 1985.

Rafkin, L. (ed.) *Different Mothers: Sons and Daughters of Lesbians Talk about Their Lives*. San Francisco: Cleis Press, 1990.

Rights of Women, the Lesbian Mothers' Legal Handbook. London: Women's Press, 1986.

Saffron, L. *Challenging Conceptions : Planning a Family by Self-insemination*. London: Cassell, 1994.

Saffron, L. *'What about the Children?' Sons and Daughters of Lesbian and Gay Parents Talk about Their Lives*. London: Cassell, 1996.

Schulenberg, J. *Gay Parenting: A Complete Guide for Gay Men and Lesbians with Children*. New York: Doubleday, 1985.

Steckel, A. *Psychosocial Development of Children of Lesbian Mothers*. New York: Praeger Publishing, 1987.

Index

This index, giving names that appear in various chapters, will enable readers to follow personal stories through the book.